CONVERSATIONAL SELLING

7 SALES CONVERSATIONS THAT DRIVE HIGH PERFORMANCE

KEN VALLA

JONES MEDIA
PUBLISHING

Conversational Selling 7 Sales Conversations that Drive High Performance
Copyright © 2018 by The Valla Group Inc

Jones Media Publishing
10645 N. Tatum Blvd. Ste. 200-166
Phoenix, AZ 85028
www.JonesMediaPublishing.com

Disclaimer:

The author strives to be as accurate and complete as possible in the creation of this book, notwithstanding the fact that the author does not warrant or represent at any time that the contents within are accurate due to the rapidly changing nature of the Internet.

While all attempts have been made to verify information provided in this publication, the Author and Publisher assume no responsibility and are not liable for errors, omissions, or contrary interpretation of the subject matter herein. The Author and Publisher hereby disclaim any liability, loss or damage incurred as a result of the application and utilization, whether directly or indirectly, of any information, suggestion, advice, or procedure in this book. Any perceived slights of specific persons, peoples, or organizations are unintentional.

In practical advice books, like anything else in life, there are no guarantees of income made. Readers are cautioned to rely on their own judgment about their individual circumstances to act accordingly. Readers are responsible for their own actions, choices, and results. This book is not intended for use as a source of legal, business, accounting or financial advice. All readers are advised to seek services of competent professionals in legal, business, accounting, and finance field.

Printed in the United States of America
ISBN-13: 978-1-945849-75-6 paperback
JMP2019.5

CONTENTS

INTRODUCTION

WHENEVER PEOPLE ASK me what I do for a living and I respond that I'm in sales, they either ask a question or make a statement. The question is invariably: "What do you sell?" The statement is typically: "I can see that because you like to talk to people." Usually, people then mention someone they know who should be in sales because that person can talk to *anyone*.

Frankly, it's always bothered me when people boil the sales profession down to "being able to talk to others." I've sometimes felt defensive; although I assumed the person didn't understand what it actually means to be in sales, especially in regard to business-to-business transactions. The truth is, I do not just simply talk to people all day long. I have complex business problems to solve and many large accounts to penetrate and grow. I have a huge quota this year and need to keep my pipeline filled. So I would think, defiantly, "This job isn't simply *talking* to people."

Fast forward through my career of thirty years in sales and I can boil a salesperson's success down to one core competency: *the ability to talk with people.*

If I were texting someone this, here's where I'd insert an "LOL." Ironically, after all this time, I've come to realize that this statement is true, and I can attest to it from personal experience as a successful lifelong seller (of sales-training-and-effectiveness solutions, no less).

However, I'll add a couple of slight but important caveats to the assertion. A salesperson's success boils down to the ability to have *productive conversations*. This profession is not about talking *to* people, but rather talking *with* them.

A conversation consists of two or more people exchanging spoken thoughts and ideas. Conducting conversations is a large part of what a seller does, but one cannot effectively converse alone. This is where the word *productive* becomes essential to the conversations a seller has. I've seen plenty of sellers who can successfully communicate with people and carry on great conversations. Once a seller finishes a conversation, they can usually tell you a lot about the customer. The critical question then becomes: *What is the outcome of that conversation?*

Ultimately, a salesperson should enter every sales conversation with a goal or expected outcome. Conversations that do not yield an outcome are not productive, and sellers who have unproductive conversations are merely "professional visitors." They are no more effective toward making a sale than they would be talking to a friend at a bar. The conversation must arrive at an outcome and getting to that point takes more than the ability to "shoot the shit."

In the business world, productive conversations take planning. They require business acumen, strategic thinking, and most importantly, making connections and building upon other conversations. Effective selling requires stringing together multiple conversations with the goal of helping your customer. This, in turn, provides the seller with the best opportunity to make a sale.

The concept of "productive conversations" is what led me to write this book. In my twenty-plus years of working in the world of sales effectiveness, my job has been to help companies measurably improve the performance of their sales organizations. This makes me uniquely subject to critique as my customers watch me closely, waiting to see if I walk the talk with respect to what I intend to teach their salespeople.

It's been through this set of experiences that I realized I'd been selling differently from my peers in this industry. I'd also been having success that other high-performing sellers were not. For years I'd been the top salesperson within my own organization. As we hired sellers from other competitors, I realized I was having greater success than their top salespeople. Year after year, my annual revenue totaled five to six times the quota of the other sellers in my industry.

I started to take an inventory of what I was doing to be successful and how it differed from what others did. That's when I identified the key to my approach: (was) my ability to conduct ongoing productive conversations in order to move each deal forward. These "productive conversations" included my conversations with customers as well as the internal company conversations required to advance my business.

Having productive conversations may sound simple. However; *It is not*. If it were, everyone would already be doing it. However, there are strategies and techniques that can enable any salesperson to converse more productively. Thus, the idea behind this book!

Most books I've read about selling provide a lot of content regarding the *what*, but very little concerning the *how*. In this book, I'll provide an understanding for both the what and the how, with relevant examples and authentic stories throughout the text to support these concepts. I have yet to come across a book that deeply explores selling strategies, so I've made that a core emphasis in this read. I'll also combine strategy with the practical skills and tools to make for a robust set of selling capabilities.

The need to have "productive conversations" ultimately shapes a seller's thinking toward building and maintaining a strong pipeline of business. It influences a seller's account strategies and guides the buy/sell process with a customer. It's the centerpiece to how a seller operates day in and day out. And, of course, how well a seller has "productive conversations" ultimately determines their success.

My intent for writing this book is to share my personal experiences, provide various examples and strategies, and suggest best practices for preparing and executing productive conversations as a way to simplify the selling role. Throughout my career, I've been very successful in my ability to do this, I want to offer my knowledge to other salespeople by boiling down this seemingly challenging sales job into something that is more easily manageable for ongoing success. I've composed this text in a way that allows a salesperson at any stage in their development and experience to obtain value.

CHAPTER 1

Laying the Foundation: The Three Fundamentals

TODAY, BUSINESS IS more complex and fast-paced than ever. Research organizations are predicting that more than one million sales jobs will be eliminated within the next decade. The workforce is changing in terms of the capabilities required for people to be successful in the future. For salespeople, this means they can no longer do their job reactively, simply taking orders and relying on their customers to describe their needs. In the modern world, successful salespeople will create a vision, determine their own level of success, and produce their own opportunities.

I've been able to achieve success as a salesperson by developing a core set of sales practices that lay the foundation for how I approach my business and customers. Just like in the game of basketball, players first need to have a core set of skills (dribbling, passing, and shooting, etc.) before they can effectively play the game. The same holds true for some basic principles of selling. These concepts will be explained throughout this book, but I'll begin by sharing the three fundamentals that got me started on the pathway to success.

Fundamental 1: Sell what you can do, not what you have

I believe sellers are often constrained by one major thing: their mindset about what they're actually selling to prospective customers. A typical salesperson knows what their company's products and services are today, then sells them. This is a limitation.

From the time I started selling, I've never limited my capacity to "think outside the box." Back then, the company I worked for had one product—a time-management training program—and that was all I had to sell. I'd talk with leaders of Fortune 500 companies in the Chicago area and try to sell this one program. It drove me nuts because while these leaders had all sorts of business issues, I was limited in what I could offer to help them. *Or was I?*

At the end of the day, I was responsible for driving revenue with only one product to sell. Let's call it a hammer, so everything started to look like a nail. Unless I started to think differently, this would be a tough road to generate sales on.

I realized that by only focusing on what my company *has* (products), and what we *do* (services), I'd be limiting my potential to offer solutions that drove customer outcomes and results. Obviously, this also limited my ability to generate revenue. The alternative was to focus on the possibilities of what we *could have* and what we *could do*, given the right situation. I wondered what we could build that business leaders needed even though it didn't yet exist. For example, perhaps we could customize what we did for our customers by partnering with another company to get the products or services that they needed.

Some salespeople may feel they have no control over the product they can offer; it simply is what it is. Maybe you're one of them. Well, hold on and keep reading.

Not everything sellers want to do with their company's products is possible, yet this shouldn't deter creative thinking. A salesperson who can visualize a future for an enhanced version of their product is extremely valuable to their company and customers. This mindset allows a seller to think freely about possibilities and have open conversations with customers to advance their expectations. The same goes for the services their company provides. When it comes to service or implementation, ask "What if?" It's important that you aren't limited by what you have in your offering because competitors will likely have the exact same or similar offering. It's the future *potential* offering—the one no one else has thought of—that can differentiate you from the competition.

* * *

Personal Anecdote

The largest and most profitable account I've ever sold was the result of expanding what was possible with our offering. The customer was a large wireless provider and had more than forty thousand salespeople. The company also hired about six to eight thousand new sellers each year and needed to train them all. We were working on a deal to provide them with sales training for this large team.

The problem was that our offering came in a package of training. Companies bought our pre-packaged training, then paid us to customize it, then paid us again to deliver the training. We charged per person for each package of training sold. This wireless company could have bought our company outright for what we would have charged them using our standard pricing model.

I started to think: "What if we completely unbundled our training package and just provided the raw content to this customer?" What if we allowed them to use their own internal training resources to design whatever sales training they wanted, using our content as the basis? What if we charged an annual fixed amount rather than charging according to our per-person model?

I worked with my customer contact and started to share some of these "What if's." I asked for help to build the business case. The customer loved these ideas. Once we got into the details of what they were already spending annually for sales training, I saw that I could actually save them 50 percent of their current annual investment while winning my own company a very large, profitable long-term deal.

Surprisingly, the harder sale was convincing the senior leadership within my organization to see the potential in this new way of bringing value to our customers. Unbundling something that had never been unbundled allowed us to resell it at a price that was greater than what we could have sold it for when it was bundled. It was a complete shift in how we leveraged our offering.

Ultimately, we won the deal. It generated over ten million dollars in revenue and continued to successfully yield measurable results for more than ten straight years. It was good business for the customer and good business for us. It produced a new model that our company then took and leveraged with several other customers.

Now, I can already hear some sales leaders who are reading this and saying to themselves, "I cannot afford to have my salespeople selling smoke and mirrors, or selling futures, or taking their eye off the ball." That may be true, but as you read this, it's important to consider what they already do have to sell but may not even know they have. Consider what they could do with your current offering that you may not have entertained as possible. Best yet, consider the new possibilities for achieving profit when your sellers can be creative rather than constrained. If your salespeople are not working this way, I can assure you that your competitor's salespeople are, or will be one day soon.

* * *

Bottom Line: Your offering is much greater than your current set of products and services. Sell what you can do, versus what you have, and see your opportunities for revenue expand!

Fundamental 2: Leverage the three types of value

Success in selling is measured by hitting your numbers. People say it's about bringing value to customers, or helping people and organizations improve, but those are means to an end. I have never known a salesperson who failed to achieve their quota year after year, but still kept their job because they were doing the right things for the customer. Companies want success, and for salespeople, they measure it only one way: *achieving your quota (at a minimum)*.

Now, to achieve their quotas, the best salespeople I've ever seen in action did one thing very well. These salespeople figured out how to bring value to customers that their competitors could not, so they were viewed by customers as resources to help them improve.

The word *value* is often thrown around today with little regard to the actual meaning. Merriam-Webster defines *value* as "a fair return or equivalent in goods, services, or money for something exchanged." Given this definition, the question then becomes: How does a salesperson (or customer) determine "fair return" based on money spent for goods and/or services they provide (or purchase)?

Just as "beauty is in the eye of the beholder," we can say, "value is in the eye of the customer." What one customer may see as a terrific value for their business, another customer may think is overpriced. Whether a customer sees value in a particular product or service may depend on many factors.

Consider the following:

- Does the product/service help the customer achieve a goal?
- Does it help the customer overcome a challenge that is keeping them from success?
- Does it differentiate them from their competitors and help them grow their business?
- Is the product of better quality for the investment than competitors' products?
- Does the purchase and use of this product ensure a level of success for key stakeholders?

As a seller, I pay attention to three types of value: *product/service, business, and personal.*

Product/Service Value

Product/service value is the one salespeople most commonly focus on because it's the easiest. This value is all about why your products/services are different and better than your competitors'. Essentially, if a seller knows their products/services inside and out, as well as who their competition is, they can sell at this level very effectively. They can even build the case for how their products/services offer the same or greater performance than the competition's for the same or lower cost. This is a true win because it becomes a fairer exchange of value when compared to the competition.

Challenge: So why isn't selling product/service value enough in today's business environment?

The reason is that today's business customers want return on their investments. Every dollar budgeted and spent is an investment of some sort. These investments may be for short-term or long-term gain, capital goods or operating expenses, or intended to help a company grow by more effectively marketing, advertising, or selling. Regardless of the reason, companies are always motivated to get a return on their money investments—which brings us to the next type of value: business.

Business Value

The second and most challenging type of value is business. This type of value is all about affecting the success of an organization. As a salesperson, you have four options to accomplish this. You can help the customer to:

1. Increase revenue
2. Reduce costs
3. Become more efficient
4. Become more effective

5.   Reduce risk

That's it! Nothing else matters.

The most effective salespeople can depict for the customer just how their offering will bring business value. In this scenario, it's not about how their product is different from one competitor's, or costs less than another competitor's. That's product value. The best salespeople can also answer the questions such as:

- What good things will happen to your business when you buy and use our product/service?
- What bad things will happen if you choose not to buy our products/services?

In my opinion , if the business value case is strong, the customer will buy from me. Because most competitors still sell on product value, any salesperson who can also sell on business value is already ahead of the game.

Challenge: So, why doesn't every salesperson just sell on business value?

The answer is because it can seem hard. Yes, it does take skill, strategic thinking, patience, knowledge, planning, and business acumen. However, it also simply requires having productive conversations. Creating and communicating a strong business value case is a two-way street. An effective salesperson does this in conjunction *with* their customer over a series of conversations. This is a skill set a seller can learn over time.

Sometimes, it's the customer's buying process that can get in the way. Check out the scenario below as an example:

Have you ever received and responded to a Request for Proposal (RFP) from a prospective customer that seemed to be all about the business need and desired results? The RFP looked to be very strategic and focused on finding the best provider to help this customer address key business challenges. Yet after you and other supplier companies responded to the RFP, the customer quickly shifted focus to product/service, delivery, and price: What does it cost for what you're delivering, and how fast can you deliver it? You probably thought to yourself, what happened? How did they change from being so strategic in their thinking?

Why does the above scenario happen? In my experience, it's because none of the supplier companies responding to the RFP could build a strong enough business-value case. And it's probably not their fault, as they likely didn't have enough information to do so. (Typically, this is really the fault of the buyer organization, but that's a topic for another time.) Without enough information, even the most experienced and skillful salesperson may fail to create a persuasive business-value case. When this happens, the proposal process and resulting conversations quickly devolve to a focus on product/service value.

The product-value-driven conversation is still important. I don't want to minimize this because short of being able to build a strong business-value case, building a strong product-value case is the next best option. If a salesperson can play the product-value game, they may still win the RFP. Engaging the customer in this way can lead to continued dialogue, eventually garnering enough information to build the business-value case.

The business value case is the key to winning more business, but it's not always enough given the third type of value: personal.

Personal Value

Personal value focuses on how you can help an individual gain from doing business with you and your organization. It answers the traditional "what's in it for me?" (WIIFM) question.

There's an old axiom, "people buy from people," and I've found that what motivates a buyer to choose one salesperson over another has a lot to do with confidence. It's the confidence the buyer has in a salesperson to deliver, follow through, and help the buyer to be successful. The buyer wants to feel confident that a salesperson is someone they can count on. If things go south, they want to know the salesperson will find a solution to fix the situation. Buyers need some form of assurance for success. Depending on their role in the purchasing decision, most buyers want to understand what exactly, you, the seller, will do to assure success.

* * *

Personal Anecdote

One of my funniest teaching stories comes at the expense of one of my competitors. A large resort and casino organization had been working with this competitor for their sales training needs. I received a call from the resort and casino's vice president of sales, and he was beside himself with anger. From what he told me, it seemed our competitor was having a hard time delivering on their commitments. When the VP of sales called them to communicate his concerns, the salesperson suggested they meet for dinner to discuss the situation. This VP of sales said to me, "I'm tired of being invited to dinner every time there is a problem. This is always that salesperson's response. I can eat dinner on my own—just solve my damn problem."

The good news for me in this story is that it opened a door to win business from our competitor. The lesson here is that personal value is not about taking a customer to dinner, to play golf, or to a ball game— it's about helping them to be successful in their job.

My focus is always to help to make my customers look good. I work toward making them feel like it was a great decision to select me and my company as their partner/provider/vendor (insert your favorite label as I don't care what they call me if we're doing business together). I've helped people who specifically bought from me gain recognition within their companies or even get promoted as a result of the work we did together. That is a tremendous feeling of satisfaction for me and also something I utilize as I work to earn business from other new clients.

Challenge: Remember the salesperson who doesn't get to keep their job unless they produce? Well the same is true for buyers.

Poor investing on a buyer's part can cost them their job or limit their upward mobility in an organization. By definition, buyers have a vested interest in the overall success of an initiative as well. This is what *personal value* means. Yet not many salespeople think about how to provide this value to the key stakeholders, let alone are good at it. Salespeople are usually more interested in making a sale and hitting their numbers. Determining how to provide personal value to a customer could be the differentiating factor in a competitive deal.

I've experienced losing an important deal due to inattention to personal value. I was competing against a company that had written a book about selling effectiveness. The VP of sales at our customer account had read the book and wanted his company's salespeople to use its approach. He asked our company to propose how we would make this happen as an alternative to the company that wrote the book.

The buyer worked for the VP of sales and was the decision-maker for who to hire to do the training. The day he made the decision to go with our competitor, he told me we'd built a stronger business case (demonstrated how we would make their sales team more effective for a lesser investment than our competitor) and a stronger product case (demonstrated how our offering was more complete and easy to implement than our competitor's). Yet we lost. The buyer was afraid that if anything went wrong (even though he wasn't sure anything would go wrong), he'd lose his job because the VP of sales would wonder why he didn't just go with the people who wrote the book—why he would even take that chance. So in essence, it came down to personal value. He felt safer in his job security even though all other value factors were in our favor.

Bottom Line: Winning business is about creating and articulating business, product, and personal value. All three values are important. Having all three in place won't guarantee a sale but certainly increases the odds. Missing any one of them can lose you a deal.

Fundamental 3: Build a cadre of Petermans

Even with the right degree of knowledge about a company's products or services, I've found that a huge differentiator for prospective customers is my ability to share stories about how customers are *applying* our organization's offerings. The focus is not on what the offering *is*, but how other customers are using our products and services to advance their business. Potential buyers want to understand the process another customer went through to implement and integrate our offering into their business. This is the information they can't find on the internet or in readily available data. This can be a point of differentiation for any salesperson if they do it well.

If buyers can find information about your offering online, why do they need a salesperson to recite it?

They don't.

What they do need is a salesperson who has a holistic view of many different customers: How they purchase, implement, integrate, and measure the return on investment (ROI) of your company's offering. This is the type of information that builds a customer's confidence in a salesperson. Customers want to hear this information, and it helps if the salesperson can share it in a story format that makes for an engaging, fun, and compelling conversation. People love to hear good stories.

The hardest part of the "storytelling" skill is that the most effective stories come from authentic, real-life experiences of sellers, and each salesperson may only have so many stories to tell.

So what do they do?

They borrow from other sellers. I've had many salespeople ask me to share my real life selling stories with them, so they can in turn use these stories with their customers or prospective buyers.

I call these stories *Petermans*. A *Peterman* is not a seller's own personal story but rather one borrowed from another seller's experience.

Why *"Petermans?"* I came up with the term after watching an episode of the television show *Seinfeld*. In the show, one of the characters, Elaine, has a boss named J. Peterman. In one episode, Peterman decides to write an autobiography but realizes his life is mundane and is unable to write exciting stories about himself. Subsequently, he discovers that Elaine's friend, Kramer, has very interesting stories to tell. Peterman eventually offers Kramer a large sum of money for these stories to include in his autobiography as if they were his own.

If someone asks me to tell them a story about my personal experience with a customer with the intent to share it with their customer, I call that a *Peterman*. Sellers at every level use these stories to appease a customer and encourage a sale, just as I have a large number of *Petermans* that I've collected from other salespeople over the years as well.

Sellers need to build a cadre of *Petermans* to draw upon as they converse with customers. This is incredibly important for salespeople to engage customers and build credibility. The salesperson who can spontaneously tell a relevant story to a customer is able to quickly establish themselves as a resource.

I've successfully utilized the concept of *Petermans* for years, and it's a great strategy. Over time sellers build up their own real-life stories and can then couple them with *Petermans*. Once a seller achieves this level, the combination of *Petermans* and their own real customer encounters will make for a powerful body of experience.

Bottom Line: Conveying knowledge and experience in a compelling story-like way can paint a vision for the customer and differentiate a seller as a resource. Get a lineup of *Petermans* in place, couple them with your own experiences, and you'll have a rich source of stories to pull from.

CHAPTER 2

Seven (7) Sales Conversations

SELLING INCLUDES SEVERAL types of conversations. Consider the typical sales process with a customer. The salesperson prospects to try and get a meeting set up with the customer. Prospecting includes calling on potential customers (having initial conversations) to see if they'd be willing to schedule a longer, more detailed conversation. Then, after the second conversation, there are either more discussions to determine if there is a real opportunity, or discussions internally about making a recommendation. There are presentations (a form of conversation since the seller does not want this to be one way), negotiations (which are conversations), then conversations to finalize the deal and begin implementation. The common thread: *selling is all about conversations.*

Sellers need to be prepared to conduct multiple types of conversations, across multiple stakeholders, with flexibility to adapt based upon how the customer wants to buy. This is the hard part. There is not a one-size-fits-all approach.

* * *

Simplify: Think in stages of selling

For years I've seen companies and sellers struggle to define the concept of a "sales process." They attempt to explain what specific steps sellers need to take in order to be effective. They publish these steps in internal documents for all the company's sellers to read. Often, they lay out each step in the process in excruciating detail, with many seller activities to be completed along the way. Essentially, they follow a checklist-type format—or many times employ an actual checklist!

In my twenty-plus years of experience working in the sales-effectiveness industry, I've discovered that most salespeople don't like or use their company's published sales process. My company had one of these documents; and I read it once and filed it in a folder on my computer.

My theory: is that these documents aren't useful to sellers because a single selling process is not relevant to how customers buy today. There is no "one size fits all." The issue with a typical sales process is that it often emphasizes the activities that the seller's organization wants, versus what's actually best for the customer. This has always been a leading concern for me. Successful sales are not about the selling organization. They're about helping the customer solve problems and achieve goals and finding the best approach to get there.

I like to think about selling in stages to help the customer buy. My approach is straightforward: the job of a salesperson is to *find*, *win*, and *keep* business opportunities.

Then consider that selling has three basic stages: *early*, *middle*, and *late*.

You *find* opportunities in the *early* stage of selling; *win* opportunities in the *middle* and *late* stage of selling; *keep* business as a part of your *account strategy*.

Each stage includes one or multiple conversations to reach the outcome for that stage. Once the outcome has been reached, I make a mental note to move the opportunity onto the next stage in the process.

The Early Stage

The main outcome I aim to earn in early-stage selling is *opportunity creation or validation*. In this stage I'm either finding an opportunity proactively or validating an opportunity via a lead or referral.

The Middle Stage

The main outcome of middle-stage selling: providing a *value-based recommendation*. During this stage I determine a solution for the customer that is driven by the three types of value. However, this solution also has to have support both from the customer stakeholders and from within my own organization.

The Late Stage

The main outcome of late-stage selling is *mutual agreement*. At this stage, I'm focused on simply earning a finalized deal. The agreement needs to be mutual, meaning both my organization and the customer need to feel it's good business for our respective organizations.

Bottom Line: The central theme to remember is that a staged approach to selling allows me to focus on conversations and outcomes while guiding the customer through the buying process.

* * *

Leverage various types of conversations to grow your sales success.

I've built a "toolkit" of seven conversations to draw upon depending on the situation and customer. These are the seven conversations I've used to help me successfully *find and win* business throughout the three stages of selling. Below, I identify and provide a brief summary for each type of conversation. The conversations are written as if each one stands alone, but I can assure you that the process is not that clean in real life. Thus, the difference between the art and science of selling. I also include examples of where these conversations may overlap or be combined from two into one. You'll want to always tailor the conversations based upon the buying process and customer criteria. Be flexible and plan to adjust.

- Early Stage
  1. *Prospecting Conversation*—Secure an initial meeting with a customer.
  2. *Lead-Follow-Up* Conversation—Validate whether an opportunity truly exists based on an incoming lead.
  3. *Learn-and-Share Conversation*—Learn about a customer's business landscape to mutually identify opportunities that add value to the customer.

- Middle Stage
  4. *Solution-Definition Conversation*—Define the parameters, requirements, standards, and expectations of the customer with regard to a potential solution.
  5. *Solution-Recommendation Conversation*—Discuss a proposal with a customer and gain their buy-in and feedback to the recommendation.

- Late Stage
  6. *Closing-and-Next-Steps Conversation*—Gain final agreement on the scope and discuss actions and timing for moving forward.
  7. *Contracting/Procurement Conversation*—Work through any final terms, conditions, discounts, or scope modifications with a customer's procurement/legal department prior to signature.

Bottom Line: There are multiple types of conversations that apply to finding and winning sales opportunities. Use them as tools to help you successfully navigate the buy/sell process.

* * *

Follow a conversation framework

Consistency is an important ingredient to success for just about anything in life. Whether you're trying to save money or lose weight, the idea of being consistent is central to achieving long-term success. The same goes for selling. Regardless of the type of conversation and sales stage, I follow a basic conversation framework to prepare and execute these discussions.

This framework consists of three core elements: *guide*, *explore*, and *agree*.

The idea is that I am concurrently guiding the conversation, exploring possibilities, and gaining commitment from the customer along the way. Every conversation should include all three aspects.

Guide

The *guide* dimension of the framework focuses on enabling an interaction that meets the customer's expectations and includes transparency. The rep's role is to determine if they're driving the process or if the customer wants to take charge. Either way, the rep should be prepared to adapt to the customer's communication style, sense of urgency, and reason for the conversation in a manner that meets them where they are. Customers want to feel in control of the process, yet want help and direction from a competent salesperson.

Explore

Explore dimension focuses on testing ways to add value to the customer. The seller should be open-minded to explore possibilities, ask questions, share ideas, leverage a Peterman, etc., all in the spirit of defining the potential opportunity, scope, or process for working together. This dimension is about determining the possibilities and realities of a business partnership.

Agree

The *agree* dimension focuses on taking action. This includes working through both the conversation and the overall buying process. Closing business is a series of small closes along the way, not one big close at the end. Therefore, every conversation needs to have an "agree" component to it. The seller should effectively summarize information from a meeting to reach an agreement and determine the next steps in the buying process.

Bottom Line: Utilizing this conversation framework is a flexible means to navigate each customer sales situation. Guiding, exploring, and agreeing are the three skill sets that will enable a salesperson to drive the outcomes they desire.

Throughout this book I provide examples and identify the *guide, explore,* and *agree* components to a conversation for an even better understanding of this concept.

* * *

CHAPTER 3

Early-Stage Selling: Conversations for New Business Development

TODAY, CUSTOMERS ARE very busy. Prospective buyers or influencers do not have time to meet with all the salespeople who want their attention and time. They get hammered daily with requests for "discovery" meetings, where the seller asks questions to build their personal knowledge and see if they can find an opportunity for themselves. Customers don't have the time, nor should they take the time, to educate a salesperson without something of value in return.

I once had a vice president of sales told me, "If I could meet with all the vendor salespeople who wanted to conduct discovery calls with me, I could spend my entire day educating other people." He continued, "If a salesperson can't bring me something of value, then why should I meet with them?"

I completely understood this perspective.

So, if the customer's goal is to get something of value in return for meeting with you, how do you do that? It begins with your prospecting strategy and extends directly into your first learn-and-share conversation. In chapters four through six, we'll explore the "how-to's" of bringing value early and often.

Bottom Line: The outcome of early-stage selling is to create or validate an opportunity for your company.

CHAPTER 4

The Proactive Prospecting Conversation

LET'S FACE IT, prospecting and finding new opportunities is not as much fun as working on existing opportunities and trying to win business. The thought of prospecting to people you don't know and getting turned down for potential meetings just isn't enjoyable. Therefore, it's easy for a salesperson to want to put their efforts toward anything that's already in the pipeline and procrastinate on keeping it filled from the bottom up. I understand, I know it's hard to do this—I've been there.

There's no magic trick to make this go away. The best advice I can provide is to be well organized and thoughtful in terms of your prospecting strategy.

I make this as efficient a process as possible and put myself in the best situation to be successful. This starts with lining up which companies to call on, who the target people are, my message once I reach them, and their contact information. Once these things are in place all I have to do is act—it's on me.

I typically use the telephone and cold call, coupled with email and InMail from LinkedIn as my means of contact. I'll change it up—for example, sometimes call, leave a message, then send an immediate email follow-up. Sometimes, I'll just call and not leave a message but dial multiple times a day or week; I'm persistent in a professional manner.

This means I respect the privacy of my prospects and do not call them at odd hours of the day or badger them with multiple emails or voicemails. I simply work hard. Otherwise, it's easy to make the excuses to not prospect, and my early-stage pipeline ends up looking very bare.

I worked my first six years in sales on 100 percent commission. No dials, no opportunities; no opportunities, no sales—easy to figure.

On the bright side, there's great value in a salesperson who can create new opportunities for their pipeline. Any salesperson who can do this effectively will separate themselves from most other salespeople in the market.

Sellers who do not create their own opportunities are relying on their organization to provide them with leads. I've never found this strategy to be successful. I'd rather control my future and develop my own opportunities, and if I get an actual lead from my company I consider that "gravy."

Unless you are lucky, customer meetings don't magically appear on your calendar. Salespeople need to first gain access to the right people and secure their agreement to a meeting. Prospecting conversations take planning and execution. I use a five-step process:

1. Research and identify potential opportunities online.
2. Identify potential stakeholders.
3. Connect your experience to potential opportunities.
4. Craft your message.
5. Execute.

Below you'll find a detailed explanation and understanding for each step within this process.

Step 1: Research and identify potential opportunities online

The idea of online account research is simply to provide one input toward your account and conversation strategy. It can tell you where the potential opportunities may lie within an account and inform you whom you should be having conversations with and why. It may also suggest that you might need to look outside this account to grow your business. It's one data point.

Information like this can be found in many places:

- Your company's CRM (Customer Relationship Management system)—assuming you have and use one
- The customer's website
- Published investor presentations, news, and articles
- Internet search
- LinkedIn

This step does not require that you sit at your computer for hours on end looking for information. I find it can take as little as twenty minutes to an hour, depending on how much I already know about the account before starting.

I'm looking for information that tells me a story about the customer's business: past, present, and future. Here are the three key questions I set out to answer:

1. Where have they been?
- When did the company start and what was their original offering?
- How has the company evolved over time?

2. Where are they today?
- Where do they sit relative to the leading companies in their industry?
- What does the company do to make money? What do they sell and to whom?
- Whom do they compete against?
- How are they structured?
- How do they measure success?

3. Where are they headed?
- How is their industry changing?

- What goals do they have organizationally over the next twelve months?
- What strategic initiatives are in place to try and achieve those goals?

To find the answers to these questions, salespeople should do *at least* the following research:

- **Account website review** is looking for the following:

  ○ Overview of the company's offering (product and services)
  ○ Press releases that suggest recent changes
  ○ Press releases on customer wins the company recently achieved
  ○ Hierarchy of the organizational structure. For example, do they have business units or a centralized structure?

- **"Investor Relations" section of the company's website.** Go to the "Events and Presentations" section and look for the most recent PowerPoint presentations from investor conferences. This applies only to public companies (not privately held). Every publicly held organization attends investor conferences in which they share information about their company to potential or existing investors. They're trying to "sell" their company to get investors to buy their stock. In doing so, they create and share presentations about their company that can be of tremendous value to a salesperson.

- **Internet search of the company to look for any third-party perspectives.** Since the website and investor presentations are created by the company itself, I find it helpful to review some information about the company from outside the organization.

- **Internet search for any recent news about the company** that would not be published on their website.

- *LinkedIn* **search of the company and individual employees.** I search for people by way of their titles to see if I can figure out their organizational structure for parts of the business I may want to call on.

Companies will share their goals online. They will even share their strategic initiatives for achieving these goals. Within these goals and initiatives there may be obvious linkages to the offerings that my company provides. Other times, I consider what it will take for the customer to be successful with their initiatives and draw a connection to how our offerings can enable that success.

The purpose of looking at all this data comes down to one question: How might my company's offering help this customer accomplish one or more of their goals? If as a result of the account research I can see the potential to make this happen, then I may have an opportunity. At this point, I haven't even spoken with anyone at the customer organization yet—this is entirely prep work.

Step 2: Identify potential stakeholders

My second step is to consider who owns the initiative or goal within this company. This leads toward the potential stakeholders. These people in turn become my calling points. I tend to start at the top of an organization—not necessarily by calling there, but identifying the organizational structure from a top-down approach.

For example, if the company has a strategic initiative to do more e-commerce through their online platform, I'll look at a couple key parts of the business. I typically start with marketing and try to understand if the company has a chief marketing officer (CMO), or some sort of equivalent. Then, I'll use LinkedIn to determine if there are vice presidents or director-level staff who report to this person. Next, I might explore their IT department to determine if they have a chief information officer (CIO) or equivalent, as well as look for vice presidents or directors below the CIO. The idea is that either of these functions would be obvious stakeholders in an e-commerce initiative.

Next, I like to start calling as high up in leadership as possible (CMO, CIO, etc.), because even if the person does not respond directly, they may pass your information to the person on the team who owns this initiative. This has happened to me on numerous occasions. I've also found that the director level and above is where larger budgets are managed, so they become my next targets.

Now, which of these stakeholders I target first depends on my company's offering. If I were working for a company in the Information Technology space, then I might start with the CIO. However, this is an example of where the seller should let their current products and services constrained their approach. The seller may want to expand their view of their company's offering and consider other functions within the prospect's business that could be call points. Perhaps your IT offering could enhance the ability of an organization's field-operations team to communicate more effectively. In that case, you might want to target the vice president of field operations for a conversation.

On the other hand, if my organization is in branding, I might still start with marketing. Neither approach is wrong and both make a great first step. Worst case, you get redirected to the correct owner of an existing initiative to engage in an exploratory conversation.

Step 3: Connect your experience to potential opportunities

The third step is to leverage any information I've found about the customer with my knowledge and experience base. I'm in a great position as a salesperson. I have the luxury of working across many customer organizations: therefore, I have a perspective that some buyers aren't able to gain from working inside of only one organization. I'm able to see how multiple companies creatively implement, integrate, and apply our offerings within their unique organizations. My ability to identify these scenarios and then leverage that experience with a potential new customer is huge.

I like the term "connect the dots"—a seller should be able to connect what they understand about what's happening within one company to the sales success and experience of another similar company. Once the seller puts these pieces together, they can begin to visualize the potential for a successful sale. I always consider *"Petermans"* and other success stories that may be of interest to a prospective customer: *"What would be interesting to them, and why?"*

This all happens as part of the prospecting plan. I'll use all this information in order to secure the meeting in the first place, as customers love to hear about experiences and examples from other companies that are relevant to them.

Another approach to consider is: *"What might stand in the way of this company achieving its goal or strategic initiative?"* Given my experience with other customers, I've likely dealt with this type of initiative and understand some of the potential challenges that may arise. Now I have something to share with this customer and the beginnings to create a new opportunity.

* * *

Personal Anecdote

One of my prospecting targets was a large cable company. I read in their annual investor presentation that they planned to partner and resell capabilities from a wireless provider. This wireless provider happened to be one of my customers. This connection immediately caught my attention because if these companies were going to do business together, then I figured they might have an interest in leveraging the same supplier.

I was absolutely correct.

I crafted an email message regarding their partnership and how my organization was already a valued supplier of the wireless company, then used this connection to get multiple meetings. This ultimately resulted in several hundred thousand dollars of consulting work with the cable company—I simply had to make the connection.

Sometimes researched information works well as a means to find potential opportunities like the example above. Other times, it steers me away from pursuing accounts that aren't likely to flourish. I worked for a company that helped our customers improve their people's performance. When I did my account research, I looked for specific goals and initiatives that required better or different performance from people. Sometimes, I even reviewed an entire investor report and found no mention of the importance of people to the company's strategy or plans. That company was focused more on other priorities. That told me they most likely weren't a good prospect for me. It didn't mean I shouldn't make a call to them, but rather that I wouldn't consider them a priority. In that instance, I'd rather find a company that publicly stated the importance of people to the success of their business plans.

* * *

Step 4: Craft your message.

The fourth step is to create a story or compelling message in order to get a meeting. My intent is always to be clear, first with myself, then with the prospective customer about what I want to achieve as a result of contacting them. My approach has always been to try and schedule a twenty-minute meeting over the phone. That has worked for me and my business, but it may not work for all sellers. Instead, you may be aiming for a thirty-minute in-person meeting, a five-minute virtual chat, or something else. Regardless, my first point of emphasis is to be clear on what I want in the end and what value the customer will gain from this conversation; then I can create a message toward that outcome.

Here's an idea of how this step may transpire.

(GUIDE)

The cold-call message to a prospective customer should start with a clear introduction:

"Hi Mary, my name is Ken Valla and I work for XYZ company. Are you familiar with us?"

If yes, then I'll ask if she's ever done business with our company in the past or how she knows of our organization. If the answer is no, then I'll quickly summarize who our company is and why it's even relevant to Mary. This piece should only be two to four sentences at the most.

(EXPLORE)

Then, I'll use a seamless transition to ask if Mary has twenty minutes for an introductory conversation in the next week or so. I'll say something like this:

"I'd like to understand your company's priorities for the next twelve to eighteen months, and also share some relevant examples of work my company is doing with similar organizations. My intent is to see if I can add value to you or your team moving forward."

I'll also insert language about her priorities as they might relate to any changes or initiatives I'm aware are happening within her company. If appropriate, it can be helpful to name-drop a couple of other companies to add credibility.

(AGREE)

Finally, I'll end by saying:

"Do you have twenty minutes to meet sometime in the coming weeks?"

This is a rough outline of a prospecting message to gain an appointment. Use this as a starting point and adjust it based on your own style. The key themes are to be brief, let the person know why it might be useful to meet with you, and ensure they understand you're trying to add value to them. Even if you have some ideas for a potential opportunity, you're not asking for a meeting to talk product or present anything. Frankly, at this point in the process, you have nothing to sell except yourself as a potential resource.

Step 5: Execute

The fifth step is to execute.

At this point I've defined my messaging specific to the customer, and now it's just a matter of taking action. Make the calls, knock on the doors, send the emails—do whatever it takes to make the connection with a prospect. Here is where it becomes a numbers game.

* * *

Personal Anecdote

The reason I prefer cold calling over the phone is because it allows me to scale my business: I can get in touch with more contacts than I ever could in person.

In one case, I literally called a prospective customer every other week for eighteen months. I also sent emails to this person. She was a key stakeholder in a large account that I wanted to do business with. I called this woman many, many times, either leaving messages or just hanging up if I got her voicemail. It got to the point where I was saying to myself, "If she ever answers the phone for one of my calls, she's going to be pissed off because I call so much."

Well, one day it finally happened, and the conversation did not go the way I'd ever expected it to.

When she answered and I asked right away if she'd ever heard of my company, she replied, "No, can you tell me more?" I couldn't believe it. I was convinced there was no way she hadn't listened to one of my voicemails or read my emails. So I assumed she probably had but just forgot because so many salespeople try to connect with her each day.

Ultimately, we scheduled an introductory call that led to multiple sales opportunities and hundreds of thousands of dollars in revenue for me.

The moral of the story is to keep calling and don't assume you're irritating the person on the other end. Assume they're not even listening and keep going until they do.

* * *

A Word of Advice

Some customers will provide hints during a prospecting call that can inform the seller what's important to them. Just listen, take notes, and let the person know you'll gladly address those topics during your follow-up meeting. Thank them, as this information will help you come prepared to the next conversation. Do not take the bait and start selling.

I've made that mistake: trying to begin the sales conversation during a prospecting call. This can be counterproductive, as I'm not ready for an extended conversation and usually try to rush. I've done this too many times and found myself talking too much, unfocused, and not communicating as effectively as I wanted to. As a result, the customer decided they didn't want to schedule a follow-up call—a missed opportunity! Had I simply not tried to start the sales conversation and just scheduled the follow-up meeting, I'd have had a better chance with that prospect.

Prospecting-Conversation Outcomes

Once the customer has answered the phone, you can expect one of two outcomes.

The first is to secure a "learn and share" meeting, which I will define later on in this book.

The second outcome is that a prospective customer will indicate that they don't have any interest in a meeting. Typically, they'll say something like, "We don't have any budget right now," "I'm busy with other priorities," or just plain, "I'm not interested right now." Regardless of the prospect's reasoning there's a critical follow-up question I've learned to ask. It goes like this: "I understand now is not good timing, do you mind if I try you back in three months to see if anything has changed?"

I assure you that the majority of people will agree to accept a follow up call.

My reasoning behind a later follow-up is that business changes, priorities shift, and maybe what isn't on the customer's radar today will be a major initiative in six months.

I use the fiscal year as a barometer for follow-up. All companies run on a fiscal year, often the calendar year starting in January, though some fiscal years begin in other months. Let's say a company abides by a calendar fiscal year. If you're speaking with a prospect in July and they turn you down for a meeting, ask if you can give them a call in the fall when they begin planning and budgeting for their next year. Being aware of their business cycle is an easy way to keep them engaged.

Then, I *always* note the follow-up date on my calendar or to-do list and follow through. I've called back hundreds of prospects using this technique. I simply remind them that we'd spoken previously and I'd asked to follow up to see if anything changed, or if there were any new initiatives for the next fiscal year that would be worth setting up a meeting to discuss. This approach works as some people will remember you, and while most don't, either way it's gone from a cold call to a warm call now.

I've had prospects say no multiple times and I continued to ask if I could follow up. They frequently say yes, and I keep calling every three to six months. It's a phone call that doesn't take much time or energy, and I've turned these follow-up calls into meetings, opportunities, and even sales. It may be the grunt work of a seller, but it's effective!

Bottom Line: Yes, a salesperson can create their own opportunities. They do not have to depend on leads. If you don't get the meeting, get an agreement to check back with a follow-up call and follow through.

CHAPTER 5

The Conversation to Follow Up on a New Lead

IF I RECEIVE a lead that suggests the customer has already created an opportunity to work together, it's incumbent upon me to validate the reality of this opportunity. During this conversation I always have my consulting hat on. The goal is to determine if the opportunity, as created by the customer, is properly defined.

For example, I sometimes meet with customers who call me in to discuss a potential project. Internally, the customer feels they've already defined the business problem, gained support from stakeholders to fix it, and determined how they want to solve for the need. They're now bringing in vendors, suppliers, or partners to request proposals. This happens all the time.

In fact, given the availability of information via the web and social media, buyers today are sometimes well down the path of purchase before they even reach out to a salesperson.

I have no problem with the customer being "ahead" of me in the buying process, as long as I can ask them to "show their work."

The phrase "show your work" takes me back to high school math class.

Remember when you'd solve a math problem and the teacher would scold you if you didn't provide evidence to show how you arrived at the answer? I use the exact same approach (minus the scolding) whenever

I receive a lead and the customer seems to be already headed down the buying path. I simply suggest that it would be helpful for me to understand the process and decisions they made to get there (*guide*). I always want to understand the origin of the opportunity in order to best help them (*explore*). How did this come up? Who was involved, and why is this so important to address? Then I'll ask, "Would this approach to the conversation today work for you?" The customer invariably says yes and begins to tell me the back story behind the project (*agree*).

Sample Framework: Goal, Implication, Approach, and Recommendation

As a consultant, there's a framework I like to apply when I'm listening to a customer.

The framework goes like this:

- **Goal**

  What is the *goal* or *problem* the customer is trying to solve? What I really want to know is whether it's truly attainable. I'm also connecting what they're saying to any success stories or *Petermans* I have to share. Basically, have we addressed this goal or problem with another customer before? If the answer is yes, then I have a strong starting point to go after this opportunity.

- **Implication**

  What happens if the company does not address the goal or solve the problem? What happens to their business? Is there a cost or other metrics to quantify this?

- **Approach**

  Next, I'm listening for the reason behind their *approach*. There are many options to solve a problem or accomplish a goal. Does their approach make sense? Is it feasible? Again, I'm measuring what they're saying in my head against the experiences I've had with other customers and determining if we have other ideas or options to share. Or, if their thinking is on target with what we've done successfully for other customers, then my experience validates their approach and I tell them as much.

- **Recommendation**

  Finally, I'm listening for their "ask" of my company so we can make a *recommendation*. What are they asking us to do or recommend in order to solve the problem or accomplish the goal? Is it doable? Do I have examples or *Petermans* to share that suggest we can help and could be a credible resource?

As a consultant, applying this framework to the conversation allows me to better understand if a customer has missed anything, made inaccurate assumptions, or is approaching the business problem ineffectively. If I sense any of these things, I will redirect the conversation and ask if I may offer some alternatives or options to their thinking. Now I'm already trying to add value to them and teeing myself up as a resource.

If I think a customer is on target with their thinking, then this tells me a couple things. First, that they've done good work, which usually indicates a degree of experience, whether it's with the problem at hand or with general business problem-solving. It may also indicate the contact's level of expertise. This is an important indicator for a seller to pay attention to. The degree of expertise of the customer contact indicates what direction you may want to take when working with this person. Typically, customers with experience tend to want to guide the buying process, while individuals with less experience like to receive more guidance. A seller should always be evaluating this and adjusting their approach accordingly.

* * *

A Warning: Requests for Proposals

Another resource for sellers is to receive leads through a Request for Proposal (RFP) from existing or new customers. There are some strategies and cautions to consider with an RFP.

In some instances, RFPs can be the "bloodsucker" of all the potential sales opportunities. They can take significant effort for no return on investment. On the other hand, they can be legitimate opportunities. I've absolutely won many, and very large, blind RFPs, meaning I had no influence over how they were written, did not have contacts inside the customer organization, and received them out of the blue. However, I've also lost a number of blind RFPs.

For years I've heard sales leaders say that if we don't help write the RFP, then someone else will—and they are the ones who win the business. This is a half truth. Some RFPs are written or heavily influenced by an incumbent provider; I have been fortunate enough to write a few. But more are written internally and without the influence of one of your competitors.

Here are a couple clues to look out for to determine whether an RFP was written by or with great influence from a competitor:

Extremely well-defined scope. No offense to the buying companies, but this is a "tell," as most procurement people write very generic RFPs. In a well-defined RFP, the language is targeted and includes specific things the company wants and does not want. The more it already looks like a proposal in terms of the requested solution, the more likely it was influenced by another provider. Most companies that go through the RFP process want your best thinking, as opposed to telling you exactly what to do.

Very tight turnaround on the response, as if the company just needs to get two other bids to fulfill the procurement criteria. Again, most reasonable companies want your best thinking and will give you adequate time to respond. Other times the RFP may indeed be an open competition, yet the rules of engagement don't favor your ability to win. This assumes it's a blind RFP and the seller does not have existing relationships to leverage.

Some factors to consider when deciding whether to pursue the RFP might include:

- The company is unwilling to allow discussion with key line-of-business stakeholders. Everything is driven through procurement.
- The RFP is only product-focused with no strong business argument for why this initiative exists.
- The RFP has poorly defined decision criteria. This is a big one.

* * *

Personal Anecdote

I was recently pursuing an RFP and was on the Q&A call where all the suppliers call in and the customer provides answers to pre-submitted questions. One of our questions had to do with a criterion listed that referred to the ability of our solution to "integrate with the customer's existing systems."

Naturally, we asked the question, "What systems would you like us to integrate with?"

After a long pause from the business sponsors, they asked the procurement person to respond, as this criterion came from him. He paused and said, "Oh, you can disregard that criteria— it's just a standard line I pulled from our template."

I thought to myself, "Are you kidding me? What other criteria should we ignore?"

If they didn't even take the time to define good criteria to make a choice, then why waste everyone's time? I'd been suckered in and didn't realize until that moment that they had poorly defined criteria. If you see this in an RFP, take it from me and run the other way.

I do have some good RFP win stories. Perhaps one of my best wins worth sharing came from a blind RFP for a technology company looking to provide some advanced sales strategy training to their salesforce. The RFP was driven through procurement and had all the characteristics of a bad process. The scope was poorly defined, but we were not allowed to call on the sales executives to discuss this RFP, which was also very product-focused. Essentially, the company demanded we present our training program on a specific date. I was close to not responding, but something occurred to me: If this truly was a blind RFP and no other competitor was involved in writing it, then we were all in the same boat with regard to available information.

So, I began an online search for information about this company. What I looked for and found were a series of published press releases about significant sales wins their team had over the past twelve to eighteen months. In each news release they identified the customer, what was bought, and a few lines quoting their customer about why they selected this company as their partner.

Those couple lines were all I needed.

I took that information and converted it to the skills, strategy, or knowledge these wins required of the salesperson. I prepared my entire presentation around their customer win stories and how we would make *all* their sellers capable of winning these types of deals by preparing them to do the exact same things.

Their sales leaders at the meeting loved it and we won the deal.

The moral of this story is that you can be resourceful as a seller. Don't discount all RFPs outright. Think through whether there is or could be a reasonable strategy to win.

Bottom Line: Not all blind RFPs are bad to pursue. Be selective. Look for ways to influence the process even slightly to your favor. It can work.

* * *

Lead-Follow-Up Conversation Outcomes

A few different outcomes can be produced from a lead-follow-up conversation.

The seller may completely agree with the buying company's goal, approach, and request for their organization's help. If this is the case, then the seller should schedule a follow-up learn-and-share conversation. I do not try to do this simultaneously with the follow-up call for the same reasons that I do not try to engage in selling dialogue during a prospecting call: *I need to prepare and be ready to excel.*

If the seller does not agree with the customer's defined goal/problem or the proposed approach, but feels the customer is open to new thinking, then they should still schedule a learn-and-share conversation—but for a different purpose. This conversation will be to discuss options and ideas for reframing the goal/problem or the approach to solving the problem.

If the seller does not agree with the goal/problem or approach and does not feel the customer is willing to listen to new thinking, then they have a choice: either pursue cautiously or opt out and find another opportunity elsewhere.

I've always worked with the mindset of "a world of abundance." There are always many potential customers and opportunities out there.

Bottom Line: Don't just react to a lead or assume it's always a good opportunity. Guide the customer to show their thinking and keep control over how you respond.

CHAPTER 6

The Learn-and-Share Conversations for Opportunity Creation

A LEARN-AND-SHARE CONVERSATION IS a meeting wherein each party learns about the other and shares information that may be of value. I'm always learning about my customers' business. This means either validating what I believe to be true (via research or other means of acquiring information) or filling in the gaps in my story about their business. Concurrently, I have to provide value to the customer so they feel their time invested with me is worthwhile.

I may have a single learn-and-share conversation with a customer to identify or create a sales opportunity. In other situations, we may have a series of learn-and-share conversations, possibly with multiple people at the same company, before an opportunity is defined.

The ultimate objective of a learn-and-share conversation is to identify an opportunity driven by a goal or problem the customer wants to solve for, where the customer is potentially interested in my help. I understand that I'll have to earn the business for this to move from *potentially* wants my help to *definitely* wants my help. At this point, I'm completely satisfied that the customer is serious about moving to the next stage together.

A Word of Advice

Goal or problem-driven opportunities can either be simple transactions or quite strategic. The key is to understand that every purchase is made for a reason. People buy food to solve for the problem of being hungry, or they buy a gym membership with the goal of losing weight. Every purchase by a company serves a goal or problem statement. The seller's job is to know what the driving need is, and not blindly focus on the fact that the customer wants to buy something from them regardless of the purpose.

Nevertheless, whether the opportunity is created proactively or reactively, there's a method to prepare and conduct an effective learn-and-share conversation.

Preparing for a Learn-and-Share Conversation

During early-stage selling I'm not formulating a recommendation, but rather starting to paint a vision in my head based upon my current knowledge about the customer and my experiences selling to similar companies. The "vision" is only a stake in the ground. I don't get too excited, as it will likely change, and possibly more than once. It simply gives me a better starting point than talking about our products and services.

I think back to the research which led to getting the meeting in the first place.

What objectives, challenges, or projects am I aware of that might be important to this customer? This is a baseline for preparation.

The next step is to forget my offering for a moment. What I bring to a customer as a salesperson is a wealth of experience with many different companies. They do not have this experience. They are inside one organization; I'm on the outside and have a broader view of the market with many customer examples to draw upon. So, before I even meet with a new customer I'm already sizing them up against other similar customers that have bought from me. Again, this is for the purpose of preparing to share the experience I can bring as a resource.

Essentially, I'm saying to the customer, "I understand you are trying to accomplish these things. We've helped other organizations address similar challenges. Maybe there is some value in discussing?"

It's a starting point and will likely evolve once the actual conversations start. This is the same approach I use to get the meeting in the first place. This mindset has to carry through to the learn-and-share conversation.

Here is where my *"Petermans"* or real-life stories come into play. Again, these are stories that give prospective customers information about other similar organizations that faced similar challenges, and how they went about addressing their needs: What they did, what they learned, and how they did it. These are all things a customer will not find easily on their own. Thus, if this information helps the customer to think differently about their own situation, or validates what they are planning to do already, then I've really added value. In turn, it also typically provides a nice segue for me to learn more because I've earned the right with the customer.

My preparation starts with this mindset: the goal is to create or validate an opportunity. The meeting plan needs to have two components:

1. What do I want to learn?
2. What do I plan to share?

Each time, I will start with what I want to learn about the customer's situation to either create or validate an opportunity. The old axiom says, "Don't ask a customer a question to which you could find the answer somewhere else." Generally, it's a good rule.

Except when it's not.

The reason I don't always practice this is because sometimes there's value in asking a question you *think* you know the answer to, simply to get a person's perspective on the subject.

Likewise, I need to be ready to share *Petermans* or personal examples that are relevant to the situation. I try to have a couple *Petermans* at the problem/goal level as well as at the approach level. This allows me the versatility to pivot the conversation if need be.

Always be ready to pivot.

The best laid plans will change, and I may need to adjust or switch topics on the business issue. My plan is to prepare for things to shift by considering alternative areas of interest for the person I'm meeting with. This is sometimes a best guess or might be based upon similar conversations with individuals from other companies. If two people have the same role in different companies, it's likely they have some parallel interests.

I use this as a baseline to prepare.

The conversation preparation should include these elements:

- What is the purpose of the meeting? (*Guide*)
- What things am I hoping to learn and what types of examples or Petermans am I ready to share? (*Explore*)
- What outcome am I aiming for as a result of this conversation? (*Agree*)
- Does the customer have anything they want to add or change to the plan? (*Agree*, again!)

Bottom Line: The seller should have the following information ready prior to conducting a learn-and-share conversation:

- Summary of understanding about the customer's business in a story-like format
- Relevant *Petermans* or personal examples (two or three in total at both the goal/problem and approach levels)
- Questions to validate your understanding and learn more information from this customer
- Anticipated questions the customer may have for you with answers: Petermans or examples to help respond

Conducting a Learn-and-Share Conversation: The Seven Steps

In the next phase, I need to be ready to execute on a learn-and-share conversation. The main components of this conversation should include:

1. Review how we got here, the meeting purpose, and desired outcomes.
2. Make introductions (or reintroduction), both personal and organizational. The seller goes first to lay the groundwork.
3. Summarize your understanding of their current business landscape and link back to anything the customer said in their introduction.
4. Ask questions to validate, understand, and gain more detail. Share an example or Peterman to direct the conversation. Be prepared to pivot at any time.
5. Assess customer's willingness to change. Is there an opportunity? Do they want my help?
6. Determine the competitive landscape and begin to evaluate strategies based on the customer's responses.
7. Guide the buy/sell process.

Step One: Level Set

I always felt the easiest way to open a meeting was a review of how we got here in the first place. Now, this is after any type of relating dialogue and getting to know one another. Presumably, there was a conversation (live or via email) that led to scheduling the meeting in the first place. Yet in my experience, I've learned that people may not remember how they ended up in this meeting. Do not assume that they do. Instead of asking them, I like to just take control and ask if I can do a quick recap on how we got to this point. The customer almost always will respond with a yes, and this provides a great level set for the conversation to get everyone on the same page. This is another excellent example of the *agree* element.

I suggest beginning with a short synopsis. Do not go crazy with information, and focus on the key actions and decisions made along the way that led to you being in this conversation together. This is a great transition into the meeting purpose and outcomes expected. At this point you can stop and ask the customer if they have anything to add to the recap, meeting purpose, and outcomes—in other words, *explore*.

Step Two: The Power of a Flexible Introduction

If the main outcome from early-stage selling is opportunity creation, then the seller needs to quickly build credibility with the prospective buyer. I recommend developing two versions of two introduction styles:

1. Organizational introduction

    a. Short version
    b. Long version

2. Personal introduction

    a. Short version
    b. Long version

The key is to read the cues and clues in the customer's behavior to tell which version is appropriate for the situation. If the customer is in a hurry or appears to be moving quickly, then go with a short version. If they appear willing to sit back and take their time with this meeting, then go with a long version.

In any case, I always try to tell a story about who I am and what my company does.

Even if you work for a well-known company, do not assume the customer knows all your capabilities, or even how your company wants to be positioned in the marketplace. This is your opportunity to frame or reframe your company in the customer's mind.

For a personal introduction style, I focus on my experience in their industry plus any results I've helped other customers achieve that may be pertinent. Note that there's a fine line between being confident and credible versus being cocky. I remain confident by only speaking to things that may be relevant to this customer and reasons why I'd be a good resource for them.

An organizational introduction style requires me to prepare an overview of our company's value proposition in a way that speaks to how we are unique compared to our competitors.

Consider teeing up your company in a "from-to" manner. This can be helpful for customers who may think they know your company but don't have a current view. It allows you to frame how your organization has shifted *from* whatever you were known for historically *to* whatever you want to be known for today and moving forward.

For example, a seller meeting with a customer for the first time might say, "Our company is an industry-leading, cloud-based supplier of supply-chain software solutions." On the other hand, if you're meeting with someone who knows your company from the past, you might reframe to say, "You likely know us as a premise-based, perpetual-licensed software supplier based upon our past work in the industry; however, given the changes in our industry we have shifted to a cloud-based, subscription-software supplier for supply-chain solutions, and based on third-party evaluations, we are now considered an industry leader."

A Word of Advice

It can be very challenging for a salesperson to prepare for a meeting and not think about their products and services. It's even more difficult not to go there during the actual meeting. The answer is in how you think about and position your offering with a customer.

When I consider how to position my offering with a customer, I've always liked the analogy of a pantry in relation to a chef and meal.

I'll tell a customer that we need to start with what type of meal they want, not with what we have in the pantry, or what prepackaged foods we have to cook. Start with the customer's end vision. Once the "meal" has been determined, then look to see what ingredients are available. As a salesperson, your job is to figure out how to make that meal for the customer. Sometimes, the meal will be just slightly different from another customer's; sometimes it's exactly the same; other times it's radically different.

I may end up describing types of "meals" I've created for other customers as a way to depict what's possible. This will keep them hungry—no pun intended. It also keeps the conversation focused on our experience and less on our products. If customers wanted product information, they would just go to our website. What they want are experiences.

I understand that sometimes the customer may want a meal that your company is not in the position of making. They may want ingredients your company doesn't have and is unable to obtain easily or profitably. Or perhaps you're not in a position to do this level of customization or configuration with your offering for every customer. In my experience, though, you'll find few major differences between customers. For the most part, you'll be able to recreate the "meal" you've made for another customer by tweaking something or repositioning how it could work for your new customer.

I've been able to take the same basic recommendation and leverage it with another similar company. I'll take elements of various customer proposals and experiences to custom-create a solution for each customer. It may be only a slight variation, but it's enough to make it right for them. It is definitely a "what if" approach:

What if we changed our products to do this?
What if we customized our offering differently?
What if we changed the order of how we implement our services?

For example, I sold similar solutions to five different Fortune 1000 companies within the same industry. These were strategic projects that drove the engagement of their sales teams with customers. Some were in other countries, so they didn't all compete directly. However, I can assure you the fifth company got the best value because I'd already helped four other companies implement the same thing. I knew what would work, what barriers they might encounter, and how to plan effectively for the implementation.

The fifth company knew damn well that I'd already gone through the process four other times, and it was a huge selling point over my competitors. They had the confidence in me and our team because we had experience but were still able to customize the solution just enough to make it unique for them.

Why is this approach to positioning your capabilities so powerful?

Again, it's because you're starting with the business outcomes for the customer, helping them paint a vision of what they want or could have. This approach is embraced by buyers who want results. From the customer's perspective, the process of getting to a recommendation is seemingly designed just for them. What they may not know is whether it's only a slight variation or far from what I'm doing for other customers. That's okay, and where the true leverage ability of selling comes from.

*   *   *

I think the introduction is a great place to outline an example of how our company works with its customers. I tend to highlight examples where we've demonstrated flexibility, scale, innovative thinking, or nimbleness. Finally, this is where I might suggest the process for working together. I will provide a brief example of how we have worked with other companies, hitting the main steps and outcomes, as this puts me in control and demonstrates to the customer that I've done this before.

After this introduction, I transition to the customer and ask if they will introduce themselves. At this point, I find that customers are ready to talk. I've opened up about myself, my company, our approach, etc. Most customers will do more than tell me about their role. They'll begin to explain what's going on in their business. Sometimes, they'll jump ahead and go right into their priorities or plans. This is great and I just listen and take notes. Resist the urge to jump in. Listen and always take notes!

Remember to be alert for the experienced customer who wants to drive the process. I evaluate whether or not the customer has the expertise and knows what they're doing. If yes, then I let them lead. If not, I'll take the lead and suggest a process to follow.

Step Three: Summarize for Alignment

Summarize your understanding of the customer's current business landscape and link back to anything pertinent they said in their introduction.

This is one of the most critical skills that any effective salesperson must develop. I can flat-out tell you that my ability to prepare and efficiently summarize a current understanding of the customer's story has been a differentiator for me.

This is different than the "how we got here" recap at the beginning of the meeting. This depicts the customer's business situation as I know it today: where the customer is and where they are headed. All that up-front research is pulled together into a story and tells the customer I've done my homework, as well as providing a platform for a conversation. This summary is a huge credibility builder.

You can leave out the "where they have been" part unless it is relevant to the conversation.

An effective summary of the customer's business situation also leads to a form of agreement. Did I get it right (*agree*)? What would you change or add to what I just said (*explore*)? This doesn't mean knowing everything about their business. Quite the contrary, it's getting started in the conversation using correct assumptions.

Here's an example of what the summary may sound like:

May I take a moment to summarize my current understanding of your business situation? I'd like to start off using correct assumptions about your business, so let me overview what I believe is the situation, and then I'd like you to modify, validate, and expand on what I say.

Your company is the third largest in your industry. There are some mergers occurring with other competitors and they're making these organizations stronger and more competitive at the enterprise level. Your company needs to retain these large customers while still growing. As such, your company is trying to build relationships with many potential customers in the mid-market space. This market is growing and is ripe with opportunities for your organization. You are expanding the size of your sales organization to hire and train sellers to call upon this new market. One of the goals of your company is to quickly expand the size of your sales team by two hundred people this year. You are responsible for the training and development of these new sellers as well as the existing salespeople.

Step Four: Questions, Insights, and the Pivot

The natural flow of the conversation evolves from the summary of understanding to a reaction from the customer. Whether my summary was completely on target or not, I'm ready to ask quality business-oriented questions. These are intended to either validate my understanding (*agree*) or to *explore* new information. I listen to and interpret the customer's response, then pivot accordingly to share a *Peterman* or insight that links to the customer's business and potentially enhances their thinking.

* * *

Insight Vs. Data

I'd like to take a moment and talk about what an insight is, and what it is not. The business to business sales development firms have been mentioning insights for the past several years without much definition.

So let's define it.

An insight is only an insight if it tells the recipient something *insightful*. I've seen companies take research articles and call them insights, but they're actually just data. There's a huge misunderstanding in the marketplace regarding insights versus data.

Data is only insightful if it's relevant and meaningful to the person(s) with whom you are speaking. Short of that, a seller is only sharing information that may not even be helpful to a prospective or existing customer. On a bad day, it can be downright misleading or confusing to a customer. They can find plenty of data anywhere, so the seller's job is not just to share information but to identify something insightful to share.

To do so, a salesperson should be able to successfully answer these questions:

- What is the purpose of sharing this data during this conversation?
- Why would the customer want to know this now?
- Why is it relevant to the customer's business today or in the future?
- What is the implication of knowing this information?

If a seller cannot answer these basic questions, then they're simply sharing information (data), not insight.

* * *

I'm always ready to adjust with follow-up questions or *Petermans* based on the customer's response. This is why I suggest being prepared with multiple *Petermans* in the preparation step.

A very important part of the questioning component in selling is that the goal is not to ask questions. The goal is to learn information about the customer which informs whether they have a need you can help address. I see too many salespeople and companies focused on a long series of questions to ask their customers. I've had customers of whom I'd ask a single open-ended question, and they responded by answering that question and five other questions along the way. Do not get centered on asking questions. Focus on what information you want to learn from the customer and leverage strategic questions from that standpoint.

The type of information I want to learn links back to the goal or problem needing to be solved. We know that customers want value, and that it falls within four categories:

1) Increase revenue
2) Reduce their costs
3) Become more efficient
4) Become more effective
5) Reduce risk

My objective is to understand which of these are the key motivators for the customer that will help me determine if there is a potential opportunity. Without a link to any business-value, I have to question whether the customer would, or should, spend any money.

Prepare to pivot

In a seller's pre-call research, they may learn or already know something about the customer that helps them determine what may be insightful to share. It's always good to walk into a learn-and-share conversation with some insights, *Petermans*, or both, ready to use.

But the key skill is versatility—the ability to pivot away from what you've prepared and toward another story that may be more helpful, depending on what you learn from the customer. The best plans always seem to change, and they should, because new information always becomes available and the best salespeople can adjust accordingly.

I focus on reading the customer's response to a story I share, and I'll either respond with another story or pivot to a follow-up question that explores more about the customer's thinking (*guide and explore*). These are skills I've developed over time with practice and experience.

Sometimes I've found out during an initial conversation that the customer was already in the process of solving for a need either internally or with one of my competitors. In that case, all my good research was not a factor. The customer was already in a different place—the "train had left the station." I'd obviously try to get my company in the game, but usually my best play was to pivot the conversation toward other priorities the customer might have. In my experience, it's difficult to slow an initiative once it's started unless you have an overwhelmingly compelling argument.

In this instance, you might just say to the customer, "It sounds like you have that initiative well under control, however I'm curious if you have other priorities you need to address this coming year?"

I've had plenty of success using this pivot. Sometimes, I'll find just as good an opportunity as the one I originally went in to discuss.

For example, I met with a global software company to discuss their current initiatives and share some examples of our experience—classic learn and share. The customer spoke about the need for a type of selling that aligned well with some existing content we had available. I began down the path of explaining how we might leverage our existing content only to learn the customer had no interest in licensing content. The only way we'd do business together was for us to custom-design training for a one-time investment. I pivoted and shared some examples of how we were doing that exact type of work with other technology customers, and the customer pivoted right with me.

I ended up with a two-hundred-fifty-thousand-dollar consulting and design deal out of that pivot.

Step Five: Assess the opportunity

Assess the customer's willingness to change. Is there an opportunity? Do they want your help? Am I talking to someone who will drive change in their organization?

The customer has to see that there's a need. However, this is not enough to legitimately say there's a sales opportunity. The customer needs to be prepared to take action and solve for the need. Let's face it, companies have all kinds of needs and challenges to address. That doesn't mean they're prepared to solve for all of them. They prioritize which needs to fill or problems to solve based on what they believe is the best business decision for their organization and/or themselves as buyers (business value vs. personal value).

Even if the customer sees a need or problem, they have to be willing to change from whatever they're already doing today. Maybe they're currently not doing anything, so this is a new opportunity, or maybe they're addressing the problem internally or with a competitor. Whether the need is net new or it is a displacement, I try to determine if I can build a strong enough business-value case to get the customer to change. One thing I've learned is that I should always be honest with myself and determine if I can truly build that case. Otherwise, I'm only fooling myself and I end up wasting time pursuing bad opportunities.

Think back to the *business*, *product*, and *personal* value definitions.

I always ask myself:

- "Can we achieve enough value to get this customer to consider our offering?"
- "Will I have access to the right stakeholders and information to try and form this business case?"
- "What would be the cost to change suppliers or implement our offering, and would it be worth it to the customer?"

I don't need to build the case at this point, just see a pathway to potential success. Without this assessment, it might become one of those opportunities that lags in the pipeline because it fits a need but there's no basis for action. In the early stages, it can be hard to determine this, but your questions should focus on assessing the viability of building a case for change.

A Word of Advice

Listen for anything that suggests the customer has made this investment before. I love to hear that companies have made similar investments with our competitors.

Remember, there's an opportunity if the customer has a need, is willing to do something about it, and is willing to consider your help. If a customer has already bought from a competitor, they've answered the question about willingness to do something about a need. Now you simply have to define a new need and get the customer interested in hearing more about how you can help them. Once a customer has already bought to solve for a need, it's easier for them to buy again.

Once I've determined that the customer is willing to change, I begin to assess if I should engage in a solution-approach conversation. This depends on where the customer is in their buying process.

Recall the framework elements: goal/problem, implication, approach, and recommendation. A *solution-approach conversation* might be appropriate if the goal or problem is defined but the specifics of how to accomplish it are not.

A customer may say they need to increase their sales revenue by 10 percent from last year. That's the goal, and they want your thoughts on how to accomplish it. There are many ways to approach this goal. Here are three examples to start:

1. Focus on existing accounts and look for expansion opportunities.
2. Emphasize increased deal size.
3. Add more salespeople to gain access to new accounts.

Any of these could be viable approaches with probably a dozen other options. My job is not to push one specific approach at this point, but to offer ideas. I typically "tee up" an approach or two based on work we've done with other customers. At this point I'm testing thoughts with the customer and sharing pros and cons of each.

I identify my job as a consultant as helping a customer find a direction. I like to say that if you were going on a trip with someone, the outcome of the approach conversation would be to determine the direction (north, south, east, or west) to take. It should be a direction we both want to go.

Once we know that, it's time to get into the details and define the eventual recommendation. I'll tell the customer that until we have a solid approach and we've weighed other options, we may be jumping to a recommendation prematurely.

The solution-approach conversation is an extension of a learn-and-share conversation that is already in progress. I'll be discussing a goal or problem during a learn-and-share conversation and ask the customer if they'd be interested in options to solve based on my previous experience (*guide and explore*). The customer almost always responds with a yes (*agree*)—and who wouldn't be interested in hearing more ideas for their benefit with no strings attached at that point? This is a transition question that moves the process from: "Is there an opportunity?" to "How might we begin to solve for this opportunity?"

A Word of Advice

Occasionally, I might ask the customer question about their interest in discussing approaches, yet I'm not ready to begin that discussion or we're out of time in the current meeting. So I'll suggest a follow-up conversation where I can come back with some ideas based upon my previous experience (actual or *Petermans*). I am *guiding* the process forward at this point. Another reason to wait and schedule a separate meeting may be that you've identified an opportunity that you aren't currently experienced in solving for. In this instance, defer the conversation to another date and go get some internal help to prepare.

I prepare each approach with enough information that it still requires me to tell a story for each example. I use *quality* and *investment* as the factors that differentiate each approach. Given these factors, I might share an example where a company made a significant investment, wanted best in class, and we delivered terrific results. In another case, I might share a different example that describes a customer who invested more of their own time and resources than they did money. In this particular situation, the customer took on more responsibility because they had limited money to spend.

Throughout the process, I'm testing the approaches by sharing experiences and outlining my perspective on the pros and cons for each one. At the same time, I ask the customer for their feedback and thoughts.

I'll even explore some numbers in terms of investment. It's always a range at this point, and I share both the highest and lowest possible numbers. Whether they have a budget or not, I need them to know the range and determine if they have access to funding. For strong business-value cases, companies *will* find the money. (Budgets are reallocated all the time, so I don't worry too much about existing budgets if the value case can be built.) I listen and observe the customer's reaction to all of these questions and range of numbers. This helps me qualify the opportunity and begin to define a sales strategy should we move on to the next step.

The best possible outcome from this conversation is a customer saying, "This is the direction we want to go, can you put together a proposal to help us?" I find this happens fairly often if I've done a good job linking to the business value for this customer and produced some solid examples.

Another outcome I've experienced is a request from the customer to have the exact same meeting and include other people such as their boss or influencers within their organization. This is a very positive outcome because I've clearly done an excellent job if they want to repeat the meeting and include other people from their organization.

There are times when the customer's response to the approaches suggest there is not a good opportunity to pursue. Typically, this is due to factors like lack of budget or access to money.

Step Six: Determine and Evaluate

Determine the competitive landscape and begin to evaluate strategies based on the customer's responses.

Competition is not something I ever wait to address. This has to be part of the conversation from the early stage. In fact, many times the opportunity surfaces as a result of the customer's dissatisfaction with a current provider. Now, unless the customer is really ticked off at your competitor, they may not bring this up outright. Don't assume that just because they're buying from a competitor, the customer is totally satisfied. I mean, they did agree to this learn-and-share meeting, and most people do not have time to waste.

Other times the opportunity is brand new and there is no current competition. I don't want to assume the customer won't explore other options with this new opportunity. I've learned my lesson too many times that customers may start down a new path with me, only to learn they decided to bring some competitors along for the ride.

Strategies Against an Incumbent Competitor

There is beating the competitor head on, and then there is working around the competitor. Either way, at this stage in the process I'm simply trying to find an opportunity.

I use a few different strategies for finding opportunities where a competitor is the incumbent provider and I believe there may be business to be won. This business may be due to the customer's dissatisfaction with our competitor, or it may be that my company can provide something that our competitor cannot or is not addressing for the customer. Which strategy I select depends entirely on the conversation with the customer.

As part of my initial questions, I ask customers about their current projects—an easy place to start. During this exploration, the customer typically shares whether they're working with another company. The key is to not be so obvious that I'm gunning for my competition. I *guide* and *explore* the work currently going on and the results or value the customer has received. I may ask if there's anything the customer wishes would be better or different. Then I listen and observe.

Sometimes customers give cues about a lack of satisfaction. Other times they get really defensive, which can be kind of funny. If they start by saying how great things are going with our competitor, then I'll respond with something like, "It sounds like that work's going great and there's nothing worth exploring—may we shift topics? I'd like to ask about your goals for the next year."

This question gets one of two reactions from the customer.

In some cases, they realize that things aren't going that well with a competitor after all, and that they were defensive about that current work or relationship. In these instances, they often quickly reverse themselves. They might say, "Oh no, there are some things we'd really like to change about our current work, it's not *that* perfect" (*explore*).

In other cases, the customer will respond that, yes, they're satisfied with their current provider, but they'd be glad to shift the conversation to focus on upcoming goals (*agree*).

How the customer reacts to these questions indicates to me which strategy I want to pursue. I'd rather not push the proverbial stone uphill if the customer is satisfied with what they're buying from our competitor. Instead, I'll look for new "white space" opportunities to help them where no immediate competition exists. This is a personal preference, but I find that most people I call on have multiple goals each year, and if one is already being solved by a competitor, then I'll solve another one.

If the customer is dissatisfied with the incumbent provider, or if that competitor is not providing a complete solution, then I may go straight into a *complete displacement strategy.*

In this strategy, I focus on getting rid of the competitor entirely and realign the customer to switch their purchase with my organization. This is the most common approach by sellers and *can* work if I overcome the switching-cost argument and build a strong enough case.

I've found that unless the competitor has really screwed up inside this customer account, it can be hard to completely displace them outright. In trying to do that, I might also leave other incremental opportunities on the table because I didn't pivot to other priorities.

The complete displacement strategy tends to center on bundling or unbundling our offering. In order to displace a competitor, I've found that my ability to change the offering is the most effective way to get the conversation started. If our competitor is providing a fully bundled solution (products, services, and likely high switching costs,) then I consider a strategy where we offer an unbundled solution and the customer has less at stake due to a smaller investment and lower switching costs. The opposite is true if our organization can offer a fully bundled solution and our competitors cannot.

Since it can be a challenge to completely displace the competition, other options do exist.

Partial displacement is another strategy. For example, say Joe was buying one hundred widgets from our competitor and now he's buying eighty from them and twenty from my company. Simply substituting us for a few widgets makes it easy for Joe to test us out.

Selecting the correct bundle or unbundle strategy is always situational. I've found that sometimes even with a strong business-value argument, the personal value built by our competitor could be enough for the customer to not risk a complete change of suppliers. In this case, I go to the partial displacement strategy.

For example, a big competitor of mine had a foothold in a large account that I was trying to penetrate. I didn't have any business there.

After many prospecting calls and emails, I finally got the attention of a director who agreed to a learn-and-share conversation at a Starbucks. We met and talked to share information. It was a slow process. She explained the big shift their sales organization was undertaking, and I shared some examples of relevant experience. This turned into a second meeting, and then a third—and so we danced.

I like coffee and everything, but I was wondering if this was going anywhere when it finally became clear. It turned out our competitor had really been a pain in the butt to work with, but the customer hadn't determined that until long after they started doing business together. They put in place a large long-term agreement with high switching costs, only to find out they disliked this supplier—big time! So the director was vetting me through several short meetings to see how I stood up. Once I realized what her motivation was (personal value), it allowed me to offer initial unbundled-solution ideas to partially displace our competitor for low switching costs. Essentially, I gave her a way to give our company a chance. We had to "play nice in the sandbox" with our competitor for a while, but hey, we had everything to gain and they had everything to lose. Eventually they lost everything to us and we used that unbundled, low-switching-cost approach to turn the relationship into a long-term, high-switching-cost deal—but in this case the customer was ecstatic with us as their supplier. We ended up with a three-year deal that surpassed two and a half million dollars in revenue.

In the end I was able to unbundle our offering, win the new business, then over time re-bundle the offering for a larger sale. Sometimes you just need to get a foot in the door.

Step Seven: Guide the Buy/Sell Process

This is absolutely one of the most critical parts of the learn-and-share conversation.: the ability to adjust situationally and guide the customer through the buying process. This is different from guiding the conversation like we've already explored. It is the macro level of guiding the customer to make a purchase.

In my experience, customers do not have a standard process for buying. Yes, in later-stage selling when procurement gets involved, there will be processes and standards in place that I may have to deal with. However, in the early and middle stages, most customers do not have a defined way to buy. They may have multiple stakeholders who they know need to be involved, but honestly, beyond that, they're usually looking for direction.

As a salesperson, I go through these buying processes with customers all the time. My customer contacts do not buy as often as I sell. Guiding the buying process is a huge opportunity to differentiate myself from the competition.

Most customers appreciate guidance: That I can leverage my experience and suggest what to do next in a way that helps them to be successful. I've found that less experienced sellers tend to behave reactively: they wait for the customer to suggest what to do next. And since most customers don't have a defined process, the customers are most likely MSU (making stuff up).

My conversation with a customer might go something like this:

"We'll be discussing a current goal or business challenge the customer is facing." I'll share a *Peterman*, personal example, or insight that depicts how we've solved for this before. If the customer likes the ideas and examples, they might say "Could you provide us with some pricing or a proposal to do something like this for our company?" To which I typically reply, "Yes, but first I'd like to suggest a couple other steps to help us shape the appropriate recommendation. Would that be okay with you?"

The customer almost always agrees to my suggesting some next steps, then I outline a process that leads us directly into middle-stage selling. To get us headed in the right direction, I suggest a solution-definition conversation. (I'll explain this type of conversation in detail in the next chapter). The customer usually responds with a yes to following my lead.

Now, I'm guiding the buying process in terms of next steps.

Next, I begin to guide anyone else I need to include to build this solution with my customer.

What I've realized is that my contacts (mostly company vice presidents or director-level people) are capable of outlining the change that needs to be made at the organizational and sales level, but they're not sure about the best way to do it. I can determine this by asking them about their plans and priorities in support of the business shift. Often, I hear incomplete answers or a lot of, "We need to figure that out."

That's my cue to suggest, "I've helped other customers implement similar large-scale changes. Would you like to hear about the process and key decisions we worked through together?"

Then the conversation goes into more detail about those experiences with other customers, including:

- Who else did they include in our conversations?
- How did we use their internal conversations to gain alignment and input from key stakeholders?
- What other organizational challenges did they face, and how did we support them through the process?

These situations occur frequently, and it's critical to shape who we talk to, when we talk to that person, how to involve that person in the buying process, what data to share with each person, and so on.

This is where I create what I call an "IF" list of stakeholders. Through the conversation with my contact, I'm listening for names and asking for the list of people who will influence this decision. The "IF" list includes all the people about whom I say to myself, "If I could speak with each of them, I would have a better chance of winning this deal."

Now, what order and context I speak to them in varies. The key at this point in the conversation is to identify and gain access to them as part of the co-create process. There is no single right answer here.

At this point I'm not recommending anything. I'm not talking product or services. I'm not making my contact defensive as if to suggest they don't know what they're doing. I'm simply offering some examples that may help them think about the process toward success. I don't charge fees for this; it's an add-on value to help them and in turn help myself. If they like my examples, we'll usually work together to define a process, or at least identify the next steps to work on together. This enables me to drive the buying process.

Customers appreciate a "been there, done that" type of seller. Not a know-it-all, but someone who brings experience and can help them through the process to make a purchase. The larger the purchase, the more likely they will want and need help.

A Word of Advice

What happens when customers decline to play by the same rules?

For instance, sometimes a contact doesn't want you talking to other stakeholders but rather you work only with them. Or they say that they know what they need to do and they'll keep you informed along the way. This is usually a red flag to me, and I consider the deal as low probability at this point. You have a much higher probability of winning opportunities with customers who keep you engaged and are willing to take guidance.

Learn-and-Share Conversation Outcomes

The key thing to remember in a learn-and-share conversation is that we're not meeting for the sake of simply having a meeting, but rather to identify or create a sales opportunity that both the seller and the customer agree is worth pursuing. At this point, the sales opportunity only has to have a well-defined goal or problem that the customer is willing to solve for and is interested in hearing more about how you might help them. This is the ultimate outcome of the early stage and can occur after one or more meetings with a single contact.

Another outcome is that more information is needed from other stakeholders to clearly define the goal or problem, so additional learn-and-share conversations are scheduled. These conversations should ultimately determine whether a sales opportunity will happen or not.

Finally, the seller and/or customer may not see the value in continuing the conversations. They don't see the opportunity or feel they can address it another way. Therefore, the outcome may be to reconnect at a later time on any new priorities and forgo pursuing this one for now.

Bottom Line: The ability to conduct effective learn-and-share conversations is critical for every salespersons' success. This is where sales opportunities are created or validated, where competitive strategies start, and where sellers differentiate themselves as a resource to the customer. Early-stage selling effectiveness paves the way for later-stage success.

Summary of Early-Stage Selling Conversations

- *Prospecting Conversation*—Intended to help a salesperson secure an initial learn-and-share meeting with a customer.
- *Lead-Follow-Up Conversation*—Intended to validate whether an opportunity truly exists, based on an incoming lead.
- *Learn-and-Share Conversation*—Intended to learn about a customer's business landscape to mutually identify opportunities that add value to the customer.

CHAPTER 7

Middle-Stage Selling: Conversations to Make a Value-Based Recommendation

THIS STAGE IS my favorite part of selling: the middle stage where I get to play around with potential solutions to help customers.

I love to solve customer problems as much as I love the challenge of doing so profitably for my own organization. Since my offering is not "what I have to sell" but "what we can do," I get to use my creativity.

I enjoy brainstorming potential solutions, testing them with the customer, guiding them through the process, and ultimately deciding if an opportunity is still worth pursuing.

During this stage, I'm focused on shifting the conversation toward defining a value-based recommendation. I also need to confirm that the solution is something my customer can afford and has genuine interest in purchasing. I always say that I can create all kinds of innovative and value-based solutions, but if my customer cannot afford them or doesn't want to implement them, then who cares?

Another important aspect of this stage is to include other resources from both the customer's organization and my own company. All my deals require support from within my own organization, and I find it prudent to include these people sooner rather than later in the process.

As for the customer, I'm always aware that there are multiple stakeholders who may influence a deal (even if you are dealing directly with the business owner or president), so I proactively drive toward the inclusion of other stakeholders in the conversations.

The main outcome of this stage is to make a value-based recommendation that my customer *can* buy and *wants* to buy. The key to this stage is to ensure I have *both* a solution strategy that can lead to a value-based recommendation, and a sales strategy that builds organizational support. These are two different objectives and need to be treated as such.

The solution strategy answers the question, "How will we create a recommendation that drives the three types of value: business, product, and personal?" The solution strategy also demonstrates how our offering is different from any of our competitors'.

The sales strategy answers the question, "How we will help the customer to buy our recommendation?" This has everything to do with the stakeholders who influence the decision. The sales strategy also helps build the personal value case.

Solution and sales strategies are interdependent, but each require their own planning and execution process. I've often noticed salespeople who get focused on creating a solution or proposal and forget the need to have a sales strategy to win the business. Don't assume you can just write a proposal and throw it over the fence for the customer to buy.

Middle-stage selling always looks different depending on the customer situation. With some customers, this stage can be completed in a meeting or two that leads to a recommendation. In other cases, this stage can last weeks or even months, with many meetings involving stakeholders from both organizations. There is no one way to do this. That's another reason why I love this stage: it takes plenty of thinking and strategizing to pull it off. This is what salespeople earn the "big bucks" for and it's not easy—otherwise everyone would be in sales!

Always develop both a solution and a sales strategy. A value-based recommendation is only worthwhile if the customer can and will buy it.

Bottom Line: Do not jump right into a recommendation or proposal. Leverage the opportunity to consult with your customer and help them determine the best way to solve a problem or accomplish a goal. This is a strategy that gains their buy-in and increases your chance for a sale. It will also differentiate you from the other sellers who go right to making a potentially unfounded recommendation.

CHAPTER 8

The Solution-Definition Conversation

IF THE LEARN-AND-SHARE conversation was about the direction the customer wants to go, then the solution-definition conversation is about the details that will get us there.

The approach conversation should determine whether to go north, south, east, or west. A definition conversation asks questions like:

- Are we going straight north, or northwest?
- When are we leaving?
- How far are we going?
- Who is going?
- How will we travel?

You get the point. It's about the details of the solution, not the solution itself. The customer already defined their approach and is looking for your recommendation to help them. They want a proposal.

So, do we give it to them?

I've learned that it's easy to fall into the trap of giving the customer a proposal right away. I mean, what salesperson wouldn't want to get their proposal out there for a customer to buy something from them? Almost every salesperson has access to a generic proposal for any of their products or services and can easily whip up a proposal in short order if requested. But rather than provide a proposal, I try and redirect the customer and guide the buying process to a solution-definition conversation as the next step.

Why? Well, for a couple of reasons.

Typically, after a learn-and-share conversation where we surface an opportunity in the early stage, I won't have enough details to solve the problem. Most importantly, I know my odds of winning the deal are significantly greater if I can work with the customer to define a solution *together*. This is the sales strategy part.

Co-creating a solution with your customer is a sure way to generate their buy-in to your recommendation. This is also a natural method for including key stakeholders who will influence the buying decision. I like to approach them as helping us to collaboratively solve the problem versus my organization "throwing a recommendation over the fence" for the customer to react to.

My reply to a request for proposal is always yes. In attempt to *guide* the customer, I follow up with the question, "May I suggest the next step, which will enable me to provide you with our best recommendation?" Almost always the customer will *agree*—because who wouldn't want our best recommendation? Then, I'll suggest arranging a separate conversation to *explore* and gather more information that will determine the details of my recommendation.

I prepare for a solution-definition conversation with the assumption that once we're done, I'll have enough information to formulate a proposal. There can be multiple conversations like this, depending on the complexity of the problem/goal and the approach we're taking to address it. Sometimes this step is really straightforward and other times it's not—that just goes with the territory of selling.

I've utilized three types of solution-definition and sales-strategy conversations:

1. Solution scope (with my main contact at the company)
2. Stakeholder input
3. Stakeholder feedback

The intended outcome for these conversations is mainly to generate a value-based recommendation. Making this happen means the three types of value are front and center. I need to build a business-value case highlighting what good things will happen to the customer's business if they purchase our offering, or what bad things will happen if they don't. I also need to establish how our offering is both different and better than our competitors, and how the customer will benefit by purchasing from our company.

The Solution-Scope Conversation

I like to begin my scope conversation with the main contact I've been working with so far. I try to use the scope conversation as a baseline for future conversations with key stakeholders. The scope of work is based upon a set of criteria, the answers to which will eventually shape our recommendation:

1. Quality of product/service to be delivered
2. Switching costs (hard and soft)
3. Timing of the implementation
4. Process for working together during the implementation
5. Resources required by the customer to implement
6. Support expected from seller organization
7. Budget or access to funding
8. Price expectation

The criteria listed above may need to be modified depending on the type of business you represent, but mostly, the concept works as is. Each of the criterion listed can be essential to determining a winning solution for both the seller and customer, but there are a few that are more critical to me than others.

For example, a customer must have access to funding, which will be produced from either an existing budget for the solution we're discussing, reallocation of an existing budget to accommodate a line item for this solution, or willingness and political power to obtain funding from a more senior leader. Regardless of whether the budget for a solution already exists or can be allocated, I find that the customer typically has an expectation regarding the price to pay for a product or service.

This expectation comes from any previous experience with a related type of purchase and can be good or bad for me depending on where my company's pricing model falls within their expectations. In any case, I need to understand this sooner rather than later in order to determine if my company is "in the ballpark" with our current pricing model. If we're not, then I ascertain whether I can build a strong enough value argument to persuade the customer to pay more than what they originally anticipated. At this point, we already know an opportunity exists, but we need to qualify the opportunity itself, and determine whether my company is a good fit based on budget and price expectations. I like to jump on this topic early in the conversation to ensure we have or can get proper funding.

By "qualify," I mean that what a customer will pay is relative to the quality of the product/service we plan to deliver. In my case, I have plenty of options I can provide, from high-end sales-development solutions to very specific point solutions that require a much lesser financial investment. I'm fortunate to have the ability to configure various solutions based upon the level of product and service we provide.

Along with budget and access to funding, the customer's switching costs are very important for me to understand. I look at selling and buying as a "change process"—if the customer is buying something from me, then they're obviously planning to do something different from what they were doing before. No matter the significance of the purchase, a change is a change. As a salesperson, I am extremely tuned into the idea that this requires a customer to do something differently, and most people don't always welcome change. My job is to support the customer throughout the "change process." The biggest challenge is to determine their switching costs and address them in my solution and sales strategy. The solution-to-the-switching-cost argument revolves around both hard and soft costs.

It's important to be able to identify which switching costs are "hard" costs so I can build a plan to address them in the solution recommendation. Hard switching costs can materialize when a customer who has an inventory of our competitor's product switches to our product. This investment may be yielded as worthless and they lose money. Another example is the customer who has staff resources trained to implement a competitor's product or service, and if they switch to our company it will cost them money to retrain.

Different from hard switching costs, soft switching costs can occur within the level of comfort a customer has with their current provider or internal process. By changing to an alternative solution, a customer's comfortability can be disrupted by differences between competitors. The variation in the way one competitor responds to problems or challenges compared to the other, or the relationship differences with a new seller, can leave a customer feeling anxious and unsettled. This example of a soft switching cost will suggest itself to me if a customer begins to ask a lot of questions about how we work with our customers, who will be supporting their account, how we address problems or service issues when they arise, etc.

I spend a significant amount of time at the beginning of the scoping process identifying the types of switching costs that exist for the customer, so I can address them early on in conversations. Hard switching costs need to be addressed in the details of a solution recommendation, while soft switching costs can be resolved by building the customer's confidence in me as a seller and in the company I represent. Customers who are not confident will ask to talk with references. I've also found that when I proactively build the customer's confidence, they're less apt to ask for references. Sometimes, though, asking for references are just part of what a customer needs to do before making a purchase. Other times, it has everything to do with their confidence in me and my organization.

Criteria such as timing, resources required from a customer, and expected level of support from the seller's company, are entirely dependent on the situation. I try to size up each customer around these criteria and adjust to what makes the most sense for their business, without overcommitting my organization in the process. Gaining an understanding from the customer for important criteria is part of the ongoing conversation.

There are two questions I ask myself to achieve the clarity I am seeking:

1. What is the maximum customer expectation for each criterion?
2. What is the minimal acceptable criteria for my organization for each category?

The *maximum* customer expectation allows me to determine the scope of the solution I can build and will still fall within the customer's potential budget and expectation. Anything more means we've built something the customer can't buy.

While I like to think big, there's always a stopping point. Even for the most innovative, forward-thinking customer with the deepest pockets, there's still a limit.

At what point have we stepped outside the maximum criteria and designed something a customer will never buy?

In American football terms, this is what's known as "out-punting your coverage." This occurs when the punter kicks the ball so far down the field, it creates a problem for the tacklers. While the punter is probably delighted to have kicked the ball so far downfield, it causes a problem for the rest of his team by opening up a lot more space the player receiving the ball has to run and evade tacklers in order to reach the end zone. The same holds true with building a recommendation that your customer cannot afford or successfully implement, which therefore prevents a purchase. No matter how great it might look in the proposal or presentation, it won't make a difference if they cannot buy it.

I am careful not to build something that might look and sound great but that I know will never be purchased. My litmus test is to ask myself the following: *If I build this, and if I were the customer, would I buy it?*

It's important that if I were in my customer's shoes, I'd decide to buy this recommendation. If not, then I need to redefine and come up with other options. I have to believe in what I'm selling, or I won't be confident in my conversations to recommend solutions. Customers are very much capable of sensing doubt in a seller.

Likewise, I use similar caution for customers with appetites for a solution that seem larger than their actual capacity to buy. This takes good judgment, but if a customer starts asking for something that seems way too large or complex compared to a typical buyer, it's appropriate to proceed with caution about the opportunity. My objective is to help the customer make good decisions and spend their money wisely.

* * *

Personal Anecdote

I once had a global hardware provider reach out to me saying they needed to pull together a large sales-development curriculum. They claimed that they wanted to license every sales training program we had available in our offering, which was about twenty-five different programs. This type of purchase is totally unheard of due the sheer cost of the investment. I'd licensed multiple programs to customers but never the "whole enchilada."

I also was aware of other customers who'd licensed more content than they needed only to find themselves unhappy with the agreement at a later date. Essentially, they'd pay for a buffet only to find out they weren't that hungry, and we'd be left with a customer that was unhappy with our company. So I straightforwardly told the hardware company, "No, you do not want to license our entire curriculum."

Of course, they responded by trying to convince me that they most definitely wanted to go this route. Again, I very bluntly told them, "No, you don't."

Another dance.

In the end, I was able to get them to understand that they'd buy more than they could ever consume and end up unhappy, and that would reflect poorly on my company—and specifically me. I wanted to help them, so I suggested we work to prioritize what content they actually needed for this curriculum and form a content strategy. We ended up winning the business away from an incumbent provider because I genuinely wanted to help them spend their money in the best possible way.

We ended up with a multiyear agreement worth over two million dollars in revenue.

I refer to the initial customer request in this example as, "killing the mosquito with a bazooka."

The *minimum* acceptable criteria for my organization tells me what we can build that is still worth my investment of time and is profitable. Anything less means I probably want to walk away. I need to be thoughtful as a seller about where I spend my time. While my intent is to help everyone, there are times when a customer wants to do something that is simply not within our capability, not profitable, and frankly more work than it may be worth. Once you work from a mindset of "world of abundance," walking away from these types of opportunities becomes fairly easy.

The actual *solution-scope conversation* itself is iterative. The intent is to work with the customer to test ideas, and to listen to define both maximum and minimum expectations for each criterion. I typically *guide* the call by recapping the goal or problem that needs to be solved, the approach being taken to address the goal or problem, and an overview of what I currently understand to be the solution definition at this point. I'll then ask the customer to *agree* or modify anything I said so we continue the discussion using good assumptions.

Finally, I transition into the questions I want to *explore* and find answers to. I like to outline all the data we hope to cover in the conversation, so the customer understands the questions we want to discuss and has a forewarning. I have found this to be very helpful to the customer.

I'll also have examples of similar solutions we've leveraged with other clients to share for feedback. This is where it's important to have examples that *explore* both maximum and minimum acceptable criteria and *guide* the customer to see what is possible. This allows me to test options and gain an *agreement* or feedback specific to their situation.

After this conversation, I document my understanding in a written email or Word brief. This sets the basis for the next conversations, which include stakeholders.

The Stakeholder-Input Conversation

While defining each solution, I'm aware that criteria specific to each customer's situation will drive the decision. The seller's opportunity is to understand how this criteria applies to a potential customer and use it to frame a value-based recommendation.

What makes this challenging are situations with multiple stakeholders involved. Each of them has their own experience, interests, priorities, and expectations. Rarely does the customer gain consensus from this group prior to engaging with a salesperson. Even if they think they are 60 percent through the buying process, I've consistently found there's misalignment between stakeholders. While challenging, this situation provides an opportunity for a seller to add value to the customer organization. This is an important part of the sales strategy.

Stakeholder-input conversations are intended to be a means to gather each stakeholder's thoughts and ideas related to the target initiative. A critical success factor is to have my key contact introduce me and my organization via email and set up the purpose of the conversation. The stakeholders should understand in advance that this is an "input" conversation to gather their perspective.

At the beginning of the conversation, I'll recap why we're meeting, how their input will be used to help inform or shape our recommendation, and my understanding of their current business situation as it pertains to this initiative. This is typically a good start and demonstrates my knowledge about their business, yet highlights the need to gain each individual's perspective.

The conversation then naturally flows to an introduction, as I ask each stakeholder to outline their role in the organization. This way, I gather an understanding of their responsibilities and how this initiative will affect them. Then it becomes a learn-and-share conversation with most of the emphasis on learning. I ask questions that inform me about each person's experience with this type of initiative, interest in how this decision and project would affect them, what priorities they have that could be aligned to this initiative, and opportunities and challenges they see for the business in the next six to twelve months. This is just a sample of the data I typically gather, but enough to make a point.

Each stakeholder-input conversation is measured against the others. I'm listening for alignment and differences between the various stakeholders. Alignment is parlayed by ultimately making a recommendation that leverages the similarities.

Framing Your Recommendation

As a buyer, I like to have options. I truly believe that most people prefer having options and don't like being restricted to only one solution. This approach toward defining a recommendation encourages a dialogue between my customer and me. This is what I want, as we should be *co-creating* a solution.

My approach is to utilize a document as a "talk track" for a conversation. This is not my final and detailed recommendation. Think of this as a straw outline of a potential recommendation based upon what I've heard so far during the solution-definition and stakeholder-input conversations.

I typically have a core option (think of this as the *middle*), then I have products or services that can be added to enhance the recommendation (*maximum offering*), or products and services that can be unbundled from the core option (*minimum offering*).

Any differences in stakeholder expectations need to be called out and somehow addressed. For example, some people may want a greater degree of support from my organization than others. I'll cover this by presenting both bundled and unbundled recommendations and frankly let them "duke it out" internally as to which makes the most sense for them.

I share my core option with my main contact and use as a platform for the next step. That step might be conducting stakeholder-feedback conversations (see next section) or moving directly to a solution-recommendation conversation (see next chapter).

The Stakeholder-Feedback Conversation

An alternative to the input conversation is to conduct a stakeholder-feedback conversation. The purpose is to share a potential solution with these individuals up front to gather their feedback. This is another option for a seller's sales strategy.

You might wonder why I would do this as opposed to the input conversation?

The main reason is that I've found that some organizations and leaders prefer to "react" to something. So instead of gathering their input, they'd rather I draft a potential solution, share it with them during a live conversation, and gather their feedback. This conversation is a terrific means to learn about their preferences and expectations because the direction for our potential solution is right in front of them.

The critical success factor here is to position this as a "draft" and simply a starting point for conversations. I don't present this as our final recommendation. This allows me to request feedback and go make changes prior to presenting more formally.

I don't have a preference as to whether a seller should engage stakeholders via input or feedback or both. This truly depends on the customer situation. The key is to have these conversations in your toolkit.

Solution-Definition Conversation Outcomes

The outcome of a solution-definition conversation is to have enough information to make a recommendation that works for both organizations. This means providing value to the customer and offering something they can buy, along with profitability for the seller's organization.

The main thing to consider when multiple stakeholders are involved is recognizing when input from two different people collides. Another outcome of this process is that you'll realize whether the customer stakeholders are united or not—and the answers will inform the strategy moving forward.

Bottom Line: Do not confuse a solution strategy for a sales strategy. Determine who you need to influence in the customer's organization to get the deal done. Remember, a co-created recommendation is far more likely to be the winner.

CHAPTER 9

The Solution-Recommendation Conversation

MAKING A RECOMMENDATION to the customer is an interesting part of the process. On one hand, I'm excited to get to this point because the recommendation comes with some definitive elements to it, such as scope of products and services along with pricing. This is when things "get real."

Alternatively, I always have a little excitement about this step because of the anticipation of how the customer will react. Sales effectiveness experts will say that if I've done everything right in the previous stages, there's nothing to worry about. Well, no one ever does everything right all the time, and new information or changes occur with most deals. I'm always cautiously optimistic entering this conversation.

The reason I make the value-based recommendation as the outcome of middle-stage selling is that it works as a great transition. Until I've made a recommendation to the customer, there's nothing for them to officially buy. Once I've made a recommendation, we begin late-stage selling. This marks the transition into the beginning of the end.

The intent behind this conversation is to review our recommendation in a way that's compelling and yet offers the customer room to navigate. While it's important to be definitive about our proposal and what we're recommending to drive value, it's equally important to assume there may need to be modifications.

This is important because on a good day, we're still in co-creation.

I always felt the worst part about making a definitive recommendation is that it can seem like a transfer of control: I'm now passing the proverbial baton to the buyer and they'll let me know if they want to buy it or not. I dislike this part of the process. I either send out a proposal as is or review it with the customer before sending it out; either way, if I sent a proposal with only one choice for the customer, I'd feel like I had painted myself into a corner. Then I've presented them with our best and only option, and now it's on them to decide. This is a bad position to be in as a salesperson.

My approach to the solution-recommendation conversation is to tell a compelling story while also suggesting some options. These are not totally different recommendations, but rather modified product/service options with features that have either been eliminated or tacked on. I may also propose an alternative way to work together once the deal is complete. Fundamentally, these are modifications that will change the solution 10 to 15 percent either way. I jokingly refer to this type of recommendation as "being cast in Jell-O," a phrase I once heard from a sales manager of mine a long time ago. (It's a fun term, and I like to insert moments of comic relief as a way to put customers in a pleasant and relaxed mood.) This is important as it allows them to feel a sense of control even if I strongly feel they should agree with what I am proposing.

There are multiple reasons to explain why I like to be prepared with options regarding my recommendation.

First of all, it gives me the flexibility to pivot during the conversation without losing credibility because I positioned the recommendation to be final. There's also the likelihood that things might shift during this call, especially if multiple customer stakeholders are participating. Having the option to bundle or unbundle my recommendation even in the slightest is significant. Customers love when I am ready to shift and adjust on the spot. It reassures them that I'm capable of getting things done even if there's a change. Always be ready and prepared to shift the recommendation if needed.

Finally, these options present an opportunity for a discussion. There's nothing worse than talking through a recommendation with a quiet group. I encourage feedback and input by having options available to drive the discussion.

For this step, I prepare a compelling story for the customer about what we're proposing and why it would be important to their business. This conversation is essentially a culmination of previous discussions and work we've done together up to this point.

Recommendation-Story Elements

My recommendation story will include these elements:

Recap how we got engaged in this opportunity to begin with. This is always an easy way to start off and a level set for anyone new to the process. No matter how many times I may have asked the customer who the stakeholders are in the decision-making process, customers may suddenly introduce new people to the process.

1. Review the process we worked through to create the recommendation. Insinuate that it was co-created and provide an overview of the stakeholders that were on the IF list. Disclose who provided input, who has seen some or all of the recommendation, and who provided feedback.
2. Present an overview of the customer's business. Start with where they've been (the last year or so is my unit of analysis), where they are currently (what is happening today), and where they are headed (which goals or problems we're focused on solving for them). At this point, I always ask if there's any feedback on my understanding. I may have already checked this understanding many times with different people, but things can always change.

3. Review what we're proposing to address this customer's business need. Focus on the business value the customer will receive as a result of making this purchase and using this solution. The business value is to increase revenue, reduce costs, increase effectiveness, increase efficiency, or reduce risk; hit at least one of those business-value options. Also, as I talk through the solution, I make a point to connect anything specific we're suggesting to the input or feedback from the IF group. This is critical because it demonstrates co-creation and confirms that I was listening and using their ideas. It will establish a huge amount of credibility, and it will be hard for them to argue with themselves.

Note: I'm prepared to answer any product-value question but usually don't highlight this in the discussion unless the differentiation of our product from a competitor's is large. I wait for the customer to ask, but I always *anticipate* what they might ask prior to this meeting. Remain focused on business value and how to get there.

4. Outline the process for working together. What happens if the customer says yes to this proposal? What will it take to get this going? How will we work together, and what can the customer expect? I typically use some *Petermans* or personal examples to explain how we've worked with other customers.

At this point I ask for feedback on the overall proposal and what questions anyone has. Then I shut up and listen. The responses from this conversation will tell me the level of confidence I should have in winning the deal.

Solution-Recommendation Outcomes

A few different outcomes can result from a solution-recommendation conversation.

The ideal outcome is the customer telling me they love the proposal and providing me with a verbal agreement right there. Since this is new business, a contract will be required, so while the deal is not official, the verbal agreement is the best thing I can hope for at this point.

Another outcome is that the customer likes the proposal but wants to make some changes. This could be based on the price, the process, resource requirements, or nearly anything, but the bottom line is that they're not going to buy as is. I find this to be the most likely outcome of this conversation.

Bottom Line: The solution-recommendation conversation is the turning point on your opportunities. If you haven't made a proposal, the customer has nothing to buy. With nothing to buy, there can't be a sale. Getting here is critical to sales success, but don't rush it. Let the quality conversations that led to this point drive your story.

Summary of Middle-Stage Conversations:

- *Solution-definition conversation*—This conversation is about the parameters, requirements, standards, and expectations of the customer with regard to a solution. Utilize stakeholder input and feedback conversations to co-create the recommendation and ensure you have a sales strategy that generates support for your proposal.
- *Solution-recommendation conversation*—This conversation is intended to take a customer through your proposal and gain their buy-in and feedback to the recommendation.

CHAPTER 10

Late-Stage Selling: Conversations for Mutual Agreement

THIS IS THE final stage of the sales cycle, and the entire focus turns to winning the deal. Now, winning the deal cannot be at the expense of the customer or my organization. It still must be good business for everyone. The goal here is to gain mutual agreement between our two organizations.

A huge mistake that sellers make is focusing on getting a yes out of the customer. The seller gets too focused on the end game and loses sight of the things that will help them get a win. They may also make poor decisions that do provide them with a yes from the customer, but for a lot less profit because they just wanted the deal. Bad business is not a sustainable model.

* * *

Personal Anecdote

My dad was an accountant, and he told me a salesman joke that has always stuck with me. It goes like this:

A salesman is selling widgets for one cent each to his customers. One day, his chief financial officer calls the salesman into the office and says, "You're selling these widgets for a penny each and they cost us two cents to produce. How are you going to make up the difference?" The salesman nods his head as if to understand and suggest that he has the answer. He responds to the CFO, "Volume."

While this joke always makes me chuckle, I keep the moral of the story in the back of my mind—particularly in the early and middle stages of selling when it's still easy to get out of an opportunity without burning too much time. I love to help my customers achieve success, but it cannot be at the expense of my own company.

The best part about the late stage is that a seller finally has the end in sight. The downside to this stage is that a seller can put as significant amount of time and energy into finalizing the deal as they did to create it in the first place. I've learned that every customer makes purchases differently, so it's best to remain open and flexible in order to navigate any changes with the customer.

Key Practices

The following are some key practices I've learned to apply during late-stage selling:

- **Be *the* resource.** As a buyer, there is nothing I hate more than a salesperson telling me they have to request permission from their boss every time I ask them a question. This immediately flags a person as powerless. Buyers want to know that the person they're working with is in a position of influence and can complete things on their own, so a seller must be able to demonstrate this to the buyer. Even if they do need to confer with their boss first, they don't need to admit this to the buyer. Instead, the seller should communicate that they need to do some thinking or discuss things internally and will get back in touch afterward. It's important that a customer knows the seller can complete things internally on their behalf. This approach will provide a lot of credibility.

- **Stay close to the buyer.** This is the time in the process to be positive, responsive, and demonstrate a willingness to *earn* the buyer's business. The customer can tell if you're excited to work with them, and they'll like the display of appreciation to earn their business as opposed to just *expecting* it. A major no-no is a lack of responsiveness. Understandably, everyone gets busy and hopefully has more than one deal to work on. However, if I were a customer trying to spend money, a delay in response at this stage in the cycle would leave me to wonder what it will be like to gain your attention once the deal is signed and if something goes wrong. This is the time to be closest with the customer and overcommunicate. Every move the customer makes demands a reaction from the seller. The goal is to not be complacent or assume you're bothering the buyer instead of staying close to them.

- **Be ready to pivot if the initiative changes.** There's nothing more frustrating than learning that everything you've worked toward is now on hold because of some new change. Your options are to either get frustrated, try to state your business case louder, or simply realign. I've been in this position many times. I'm not going to say this is easy because it's not; it's downright maddening. Yes, it may feel like starting over (except for the credibility you have already built), but it's better to flex than to continue pushing something that isn't going to happen. Many times, the customer appreciates your willingness to do this. It saves them from a little personal embarrassment because they had to stop or completely shut down the first opportunity. Be willing to help them, as it can pay huge dividends.

- **If at any point things do not make sense business wise, then walk away.** I once won a deal where we got agreement, had a contract in process for signature, and were ready to start the work, only to find out the customer wanted to change the scope. They literally agreed to pay for one level of services but immediately flipped on us during the final steps and wanted quite a bit more for the same price. This didn't happen in procurement, but rather with the stakeholders I'd been working with all along. I started to figure out whether we could provide this new expected level of service for the agreed-upon price. I figured we were so close that it would stink to walk away. But after allowing myself a day to clear my head, I walked away from the deal. It definitely hurt, but I was likely dodging a bullet. Think about it: If they'd do this to us last-minute, then what was going to happen the next week or month? It was better business to go find another customer than to move forward. It was a tough call, but once I found my next opportunity, that customer became a distant memory.

Bottom Line: At this point, the buying process can go in a number of different directions. There are some key practices that will enable success. Stay flexible, adjust to the customer, and use these conversations to proactively guide the process toward mutual agreement.

CHAPTER 11

The Closing-and-Next-Steps Conversation

THE INTENT OF this conversation is to gain a final agreement on the solution scope and discuss the actions and timing to move forward. I've found that even the customers who provide a verbal yes to a recommendation at the end of the middle stage will still require actions to cement the deal. Typically, there are some changes to the scope that need to be ironed out. Having sold for nearly thirty years, I've never sent a proposal for fifty thousand dollars or more to a new customer and had them immediately agree, sign the contract, and move forward without asking a single question.

This conversation is a give and take about the scope of the solution. Customers may need to make adjustments to accommodate budgets or other stakeholders' interests. These adjustments could be substantive or moderate. This is a "mini" solution-definition conversation. The exact same preparation and execution applies.

I approach this conversation as if the deal is already won and we're simply working out the details. This is the truth, and my behavior and language need to reflect this.

Essentially, this conversation is set up to answer any remaining questions the customer has and to *explore* how I intend to *guide* them throughout the implementation process. They are especially interested in how we will get started and *agree* on next steps. The technique is to nail down differences in criteria, expectation, and scope then reflect this in an updated recommendation.

Any changes in the scope will depend on the customer and context of the situation. Sometimes we get to this point and certain criteria has become more important to the deal than it was before. When this happens, I focus on gaining alignment from the customer in order to redefine the criteria and expectations, then adjust the scope accordingly.

A productive approach is to anticipate what questions a buyer may have prior to making the decision and proactively answer them. This removes the seller from the reactionary mode. I'd rather guide than be guided. I'll share some examples of how we've helped other buyers at this stage to make a good decision.

There isn't anything that surprises me anymore. I'm even prepared for a customer who originally indicated they had the budget to buy now have to reduce their investment by 20 percent. There's also the customer who suddenly needs to have a certain product/service included that we already agreed to remove in previous discussions. I've learned that this is all just part of the selling process. Things will absolutely change as we get closer to mutual agreement, and maybe more than I anticipated.

If the customer is asking for a price reduction, I'm happy to oblige by reducing the scope. This is an easy way to answer to any request for a lesser price, as the customer will continue to get what they pay for.

Sometimes, requests from a customer lead me to get to the "question behind the question." I've had customers ask out of the blue if we can reduce our price by 25 percent even after we've made a verbal agreement. A question like that at this point in the process can really irritate me. However, after asking the customer why they're asking this question at this point, I might discover it's more about payment terms and timing rather than how much they're paying. Specifically, one customer did not have enough money in their near-term budget to cover when we'd be invoicing and collecting payment. It was more about *when* they pay, versus *what* they pay, and I can deal with that. To resolve a case like this, a solution would be to adjust the payments for a period of time or extend the payment terms. That keeps the price at the same number; we just receive our money a little later. This is an entirely different situation from reducing a price by 25 percent from the original asking, and an example of why it's useful to get to the "question behind the question."

It's possible that a customer will want to go through a few more steps before finalizing a deal. Examples of these steps include speaking with references or reviewing terms and conditions of a legal contract. No matter what the step entails, it's all indicative of good buying signals and tasks I anticipate happening anyway.

A Word of Advice

It's a good idea to distinguish between the pre-sale and post-sale conversations. Something to identify is the difference between what the customer really needs to know or understand prior to signing the deal and what things can wait until we have an actual deal in place. It might be obvious to you that asking certain questions or proposing certain activities should come after the deal is signed, but for a customer, maybe not so much. Remember, you have experience and a perspective that your customer might not have. Diffuse the situation by referencing previous situations and suggest addressing these questions once the implementation or delivery begins.

Typically, the customer will realize they're being overanalytical and can wait to confront those things. Refocus the customer on the conversation as it relates to what it will take to get them comfortable to sign off on the contract. Everything else can wait.

Do not ignore the questions or requests that can be handled post-sale. Acknowledge these concerns and inquiries, take note, and explain how you or your company will address these questions for them once the deal gets going.

I've had buyers who ask to see a project plan before signing off on the deal. My response to them is usually something along the lines of:

"The project plan is a core starting point for our work together. We anticipate that it will occur immediately once we finalize the contract. We like to wait until this point to ensure that the scope of what we plan to do together is clearly defined and signed off on by both companies. This will ensure that we capture everything required in the project plan."

Customers start to ask questions in this stage to satisfy their need to make a good decision. This is a good thing because questions demonstrate interest, while silence does not. Think about the times when you've made a significant purchase and what went through your head as a buyer as you tried to make the final decision.

Typically, our minds naturally go to a place of "What could go wrong?" As a buyer, we want to know what risks or challenges lie ahead in order to make the right decision. Therefore, buyers start to ask questions about price to ensure they're getting the best price for their investment. Buyers start to look at all of the potential internal risks and need assurances or clarity before making the purchase. The larger the purchase, and the higher the switching costs once they decide, the more questions they may bring up.

Often, these are questions you've already answered at an earlier stage. In the late stage it's easy for any seller to become frustrated. You want a yes, but the buyer starts to request more of you. I advise you to remain patient and think about it this way: If you were in their shoes, what would you be doing or asking? Consider how you'd be feeling at this point and use this as your litmus test. Be grateful they're asking questions at this point because it's a buying signal, not a bother.

I'll usually address how we plan to work together and the things we need to start working on to meet any timeline requests, such as a contract, generating a purchase order, or scheduling a project planning meeting. Of course, these actions are dependent on the type of deal, but every deal has some obvious steps to follow once the agreement is in place. I focus on all of this during the conversation as if the deal is totally done. It's a forward-looking strategy.

Something I have noticed is that a buyer may be getting questions from other people within their organization about the deal. In turn, they may ask me the question, but will rarely say it is on the behalf of someone else. For instance, the contact will ask about how we ensure success, even though I probably answered this question multiple times already. This will leave me to wonder why it is being asked again, and usually it is because someone else is asking my contact and they would prefer I answer it rather than them. I always keep this in the back of my mind because my intent is to help them be internally successful. No matter the origin, questions during any point of the process are good.

Sometimes the buyer's questions that are based on potential concerns need to be addressed after the call. This requires me to do some more work to get them the answer or information they need and circle back to this conversation another time. A key is to set specific timing to get them the information needed and get the next conversation on the calendar.

Scope changes and additional actions at this point in the process can seem like they take us backwards. It's okay because without reframing the scope or answering these requests the deal will be stalled. Always assume there will be changes in scope and therefore you are always ready.

Closing-and-Next-Steps Conversation Outcomes

The closing-and-next-steps conversation may take more than one time to finalize. The intended outcome is to secure a final agreement on the solution scope as it relates to the driving value for a customer. Then you can determine the next steps moving forward.

As a result of this conversation, I expect a verbal agreement and will revise and resubmit the proposal or contract with any new changes.

Bottom Line: Even verbal agreements require some closing and continuing steps to consummate the deal. Just focus on moving forward and not backward in the conversation. Instill confidence within the customer that you and your organization are ready to continue.

CHAPTER 12

The Contracting-and-Procurement Conversation

HONESTLY, I'D RATHER have a stick in the eye than have to conduct conversations with procurement people. No offense to any specific procurement people, but it's just one of those things I have to do, and yet the best thing that can happen is the deal that I feel I've earned anyway. Alternatively, in some cases the procurement people can hurt my chances of winning a deal, so I need to be smart about approaching this conversation.

Today, it's very common for customers in larger companies to have procurement teams that are solely responsible for contracting and ensuring their organization pays a fair rate for products or services purchased. I get it, and I understand it, but that does not mean I have to like it.

The best advice I have for dealing with procurement people connects back to the three types of value. If I've built a strong enough business case with the customer's key stakeholders, then I can remain firm on my pricing as the procurement person tries to negotiate.

One huge mistake can be forgetting how you arrived at this point with your key stakeholders. This is a result of butting heads with the procurement people, whose only goal is to reduce your price before a contract is signed. Most procurement teams will aim to reduce costs by a certain percentage, such as 10 percent.

* * *

Personal Anecdote

I once worked with a large retail organization on a strategic initiative. For months we worked with their business leaders to define the business needs and associated case. We had a strong ROI case drafted, an appropriate offering for their organization, and a defined plan to make sure all the relevant stakeholders looked good throughout the implementation. Business, product, and personal value—check, check, and check!

Enter the procurement person.

This guy wanted to negotiate a better price (ultimately 10 percent less) for the exact same deliverables. When I'm dealing with a customer, my default response to this request is to say, "Sure, let's look at what we can change in terms of the scope to reduce your investment." Most people will get to a point where we cannot simply change the price. If the investment is truly too much, then we need to reshape and provide less in our offering to them. But in this case, the procurement person wanted the exact same offering from us for a lower price. However, I already knew that the line-of-business stakeholders loved the solution we proposed and had the money budgeted for the amount we were asking, so there was no reason to change.

Trying to intimidate me, the procurement person continued to ask for the lower price and threatened to walk away if we did not oblige. He argued that his organization would send the project out to bid again, but I knew this was an idle threat because it would take months for this to happen, and his internal leaders would not be willing to wait. He wanted us to guarantee results, and if we didn't meet those expectations then they'd pay less. My response to this was: "Sure, we'd be glad to do pay-for-performance work, as long as we can charge more when the results are better than expected." Of course, he didn't want to agree to that knowing it would put his organization at risk of paying more, so I explained to him that risk-and-reward agreements can go both ways. He dropped the idea pretty quickly after that, and I continued to stand my ground on pricing.

The procurement person went back to their internal leadership in an attempt to convince them to go with another provider. He returned to his internal leadership and explained that we weren't willing to negotiate. Technically, he was correct because the true negotiation process had already taken place in the earlier stages of the buying process by the very people that held the budget and were accountable for this project. This particular procurement person was clearly late to the game and had zero influence on the decision— considering the decision to work with us for that price had been made prior to his involvement.

In the end, he signed the agreement as is.

This experience completely reinforced my thinking regarding value and gaining agreement from the right stakeholders through productive conversations in the early and middle stages of selling. By the time the deal arrives at the late stage, the scope of the agreement is already mutually agreed upon, and this can be difficult for the procurement team to undo.

* * *

I would treat any conversation like this as a solution-recommendation conversation. The only difference in this scenario would be to eliminate the review of the process describing how an opportunity was obtained or how the recommendation was formulated. This is because a procurement person does not care about any of this detail. Instead, I'll lead right into the solution, value to be gained, and the process for moving forward. I then let them ask questions from there.

I'm always prepared to explain how our pricing aligns with other competitors. Every seller should know the industry benchmark for the products or services they sell and know exactly where their standard pricing falls in comparison.

I can justify why something might be priced higher than what a procurement person would expect, or what options are available to adjust the scope. I'll imply that there are options to reduce the investment if the scope is modified in some way. Of course, the procurement person never wants to hear this because they just want the same scope for a lesser price. That's why it's important to set the expectation that a change in price will mean a change in the scope. The litmus test for holding firm on pricing is contingent on the value case and stakeholder support. In experiences like the one I described above, having the requisite support is what assured me that I had a strong position.

There are times when the procurement person can hold up or kill a deal because of internal political positioning. Usually my contact will tell me outright that we're in trouble if we don't play along, and at that point I'll agree to give up a few points in margin or price as a first-time piece of business. I always want something back for my concession, and in the worst case, the procurement conversation is a give and take. Do not just give, and if you do, be thoughtful about something they can give back. For example, I'll sometimes ask that the customer be a reference for us once we've shown them the value.

Contracting/Procurement Conversation Outcomes

The best possible outcome from this conversation is a mutually beneficial agreement on the scope and price. Sometimes it's okay to give a little, but always get something worthwhile in return. This is business, and the best sellers figure out a profitable way to get these deals done.

An alternative outcome might entail a procurement person wanting to circle back with my buyer for more internal discussions on scope. This will often happen when I'm standing firm on price and we come to a standstill. The procurement person figures that by going back to my buyer, they can elongate the process or they'll somehow be able to change the scope—which almost never happens, as the scope is the scope. In turn, I'll ask my contact how much political power the procurement person has as a way to determine if I need to make a concession to get the deal done or I should continue to stand firm. Buyers want to get the deal done just as much as the seller and become frustrated with their own procurement process. As a result, they will likely help me by sharing useful information.

Bottom Line: Procurement conversations are part of getting most deals done these days. Proper value-centered recommendations are essential to standing your ground versus negotiating on price. If the price changes, so should the scope.

Summary of Late-Stage Selling Conversations:

- *Closing-and-Next-Steps Conversation*—This conversation may be combined with solution-recommendation conversations for certain situations. The intent of the conversation is to gain final agreement on the scope and discuss actions and timing for moving forward.
- *Contracting/Procurement Conversation*—This conversation may occur prior to closing and next steps with your buyer. The intent is to work through any final terms, conditions, discounts, or scope modifications prior to signature.

CONCLUSION

SELLING IS A complex job. Anyone who says otherwise has never sold. It takes skills, knowledge, and experience to be successful, but mostly mental fortitude. This is coming from a guy who literally got walked out of my first-ever sales call by my customer as if I were my ninety-year-old grandmother. I choked so bad during that first sales call that I was sweating bullets and couldn't even finish my sentences. The customer was nice enough to take me to a coffee room, get me some water, and then escort me to the office door as if I'd just had major surgery and might fall over. He gave me a pat the back as I left the office and told me "It will get better as you get more experience."

He was right, and I actually made a nice sale on my next customer meeting a few days later. Of course, this came after a ton of practice with my boss!

While selling is complex and mentally tough, there are ways to simplify. Just like the saying, "You eat an elephant one bite at a time," you make a sale one conversation at a time. A seller can make this easier to do by focusing on the right conversations at the right times with the right customers.

In the end, selling is about talking with people. That is how business gets done today and will for the foreseeable future. Regardless of advances in technology, people still need to converse with one another, and this remains the skill that determines the degree of success each salesperson will attain.

Talking with people. Conversing effectively, productively.
Yes, it really can be that simple.

Made in the USA
Middletown, DE
17 November 2020